From
NEVER-MIND
to
EVER-MIND

From
NEVER-MIND
to
EVER-MIND

Transforming the Self
to Embrace Miracles

ROBERT ROSENTHAL, MD

Published by Gildan Media LLC
aka G&D Media.
www.GandDmedia.com

FIRST EDITION: 2019
FIRST PAPERBACK EDITION: 2021

Front cover design by David Rheinhardt of Pyrographx

Interior design by Meghan Day Healey of Story Horse, LLC.

Library of Congress Cataloging-in-Publication Data is available upon request

ISBN: 978-1-7225-0535-6

10 9 8 7 6 5 4 3 2 1

For my mother, Vivian Greenberg,
whose unconditional love and support allowed me
to become the person I am and who set the bar as
the first published writer in the family. Thank you, Mom,
for your wisdom, your warmth, your empathy, and all you've
given to so many. I am grateful beyond words. Truly.

And

For Judy Skutch Whitson, mother in another sense,
who introduced me to *A Course in Miracles* and steered
me with uncanny precision toward all of those spiritual
experiences and opportunities that turned out to be
so formative in my life. I am grateful to join you on this
journey without distance to a goal that has never changed.

Contents

Introduction

Writing about *A Course in Miracles* is not an easy or straightforward task. It may well be the most challenging spiritual system of all to unpack and explain. The reason for this is that the Course in its essence is simple, but our resistance to hearing its message is intense.

The core teaching of *A Course in Miracles* is perfectly summarized in a mere three lines from its introduction.

Nothing real can be threatened
Nothing unreal exists.
Herein lies the peace of God.[1]

The remainder of the Course—all 1249 pages (in English), which includes a Text, Workbook for Students, and Manual for Teachers—expounds on this central idea, revisiting it in multiple ways, and making use of new and seemingly different contexts to help the student understand it and apply it to her life.

The Course is holographic, and I am not just using the word as a metaphor. In a holographic photograph, any small piece cut out from the original image retains the entire image. Likewise, in the Course, the central idea appears not only in each chapter and lesson, but very often in each paragraph or even in a single, well-phrased line. Therefore, when writing about the Course, repetition and circularity become unavoidable. And yet, doesn't repetition lie at the heart of all learning? If you happened to stumble on those three lines from the Course's introduction, you might recognize their profound truth. You might post them on social media for your friends. But you would not *learn* from them. The power and artistry of *A Course in Miracles* lies in its ability to keep us engaged in the learning process by offering many variations on its central theme. We do not grow bored. We do not become habituated. Each insight comes to us as if it were fresh. And as a result, we *do* learn.

*   *   *

From Never-Mind to Ever-Mind: Transforming the Self to Embrace Miracles is the first in a series of books I will be writing to help explain the principles of *A Course in Miracles* to a diverse group of readers: those who may have heard of it, but know nothing about its teachings; those who have given it a go and given up, whether because its language seemed too difficult or its use of Christian terminology too off-putting; and those who are already studying it, but seek a deeper understanding or an easier way to communicate its ideas to family and friends. I believe this book has something important to offer to each group. For new students, certain concepts may prove radical and difficult to accept, while Course veterans may accuse me of glossing over, or omitting entirely, what they consider key teachings. I remind them that this is only the first book of a series and ask them to be patient, please.

A Course in Miracles was first published in an informal, four-volume, photocopied paperback in 1975, with a conventional three-volume hardback edition following a year later. As of this writing, over three million copies have been sold, the majority in English, but with perhaps one million in its twenty-six (and counting) foreign translations. There are over four hundred books in print discussing it. Most assume some knowledge of the Course on the part of the reader. Some quote extensively from it, trying to convey its teachings in its own words. Others attempt to simplify the Course, distilling it down to its basics, but at the risk of overlooking important concepts. And there are a few that try to guide the reader through its Text and Workbook with paragraph-by-paragraph commentary.

My goal in writing *From Never-Mind to Ever-Mind* is different. I hope to convey the Course's core principles without relying too much on its specific language and terminology, but rather to view it through the lenses of psychology, neurobiology, metaphor, and common-sense experience. If you understand the principles up front, you will be spared having to wrestle with its sometimes difficult language. I will cite many Course quotations, which I will place *in italics* to distinguish them from non-Course quotations. But only rarely will I analyze or explain them. I offer them more as sidebars, as ways to reflect on the ideas under discussion using the Course's own words. In this way, I hope to make *A Course in Miracles* both more accessible and more comprehensible. For all but the first and last chapters, I have also included specific practices designed to help you apply what you're reading to your own life in a direct and personal way.

But let's be clear. This book does not and cannot substitute for the remarkable teaching-learning program the Course provides. That you must experience for yourself. This book can, however, serve as an introduction and guide, much as a travel guidebook can allow you to successfully navigate a visit to a foreign country and develop an appreciation for its language and culture. You can see the sights and go back to your old life enriched, or you might become so captivated that you return again and again, eventually deciding to spend some extended time there or even make it your permanent home.

* * *

There is little doubt that *A Course in Miracles* is an attempt to clarify the teachings of Jesus of Nazareth and to bring those teachings in line with their original meaning by cutting through centuries of distortion and misrepresentation. To this end, the Course redefines many common Christian terms—like *Christ, Son of God, Heaven, sin, forgiveness,* even *crucifixion*—giving them wholly different meanings that are more congruent with nondual Eastern spiritual traditions than with conventional Christianity. But for too many of us, this results in a steep learning curve as we struggle to overcome old beliefs and prejudices while simultaneously grappling to comprehend the Course's unorthodox worldview. As a Jew, I certainly first approached the Course with a good deal of skepticism; for those with strict Catholic upbringings, the conflict can be greater still.

I was introduced to the Course at the age of twenty. My first reaction was mixed, and I might never have persisted in studying it had I not experienced a number of highly unusual, synchronistic events that I could only describe as miracles. I am now over sixty. I have been practicing the Course's teachings on and off for decades, trying not just to learn them, but to live them with consistency. I'm still working at it. I recently accepted the position of co-president of the Foundation for Inner Peace, the organization specifically tasked by the Voice that dictated the Course with publishing, distributing, and discussing it. Consider this book the start of such a discussion. I feel called to share what I've learned over the years, and I feel privileged to offer it to you. But I could not have written this without the benefit of all that came before, and of my mentors Bill Thetford and Judith Skutch Whitson, whose impact on my life cannot be adequately expressed in words.

The ideas you will encounter in *From Never-Mind to Ever-Mind* are powerful—radical, subversive. Like the Course from which they come, they are designed to shake up your world, but much more than that—to make it recede altogether and usher you into an entirely different state of mind, one in which fear is banished and love becomes your consistent reality. Therefore I must ask you here, at the beginning, to bear with me. These ideas can be challenging and tough to grasp. They take everything you thought you knew about yourself and the world and turn it upside down. As a result, at some point—I can almost guarantee it—a part of your mind will grow upset, possibly furious, and try very hard to convince you that the Course and its ideas are nothing but absurd nonsense which you should promptly and soundly reject. You may well be tempted to toss the book in the trash or give it to someone you're not terribly fond of.

Whenever you reach this point—the point at which your ego tears off its oh-so-reasonable disguise and storms out of hiding to smack you, shame you, intimidate you, and shove you back into line—you can be sure that you're making real progress. You're on your way to achieving something important. You've taken the first step toward allowing miracles into your life. You have opened your mind to a new path: a better way, an approach that *actually works* to bring you lasting happiness and peace of mind that's not dependent on anyone or anything outside of you. So please, do not give up on yourself. Do not give up on the love that lies waiting for you at the heart of your being.

The Happiness Game

If there is one truth that applies universally to all humans, it is that we want to be happy. We want happiness not only for ourselves, but for those we love as well. Yet no matter how content we seem to be—no matter how well things happen to be going at any given moment—we can always point to some area of our lives that could be better. Which is to say, *we never achieve perfect, abiding happiness.* We always think that if only something were different, we would be happier. As *A Course in Miracles* puts it, we seek, but we do not find. And that, perhaps, is the great human tragedy.

I am a retired board-certified psychiatrist and psychotherapist with over thirty years of clinical experience. I have worked with individuals in wonderful marriages who were plagued with poor health or financial setbacks. I have worked with highly successful corporate executives whose personal relationships were a mess—lacking in warmth, bereft of intimacy, and fraught with perpetual conflict. I have worked with individuals struggling to overcome chronic pain or fatigue, for whom the simple task of getting out of bed in the morning and smiling as their kids trotted off to school was a major triumph of will. I have worked with misers and philanthropists, each of whom prided themselves on their achievements, yet remained devastatingly unfulfilled. Well, that's life; no one can have it all, or so we like to tell ourselves. But is this really the case? What if you *could* have it all—only not in the way you think?

I would estimate that 99 percent of people, if asked, could tell you *exactly* what they think is missing from their lives—what they would need to be happy forever. I'm willing to bet that you're one of them. I used to be one of those people too. I studied metaphysical systems that promised to show me how to manifest my heart's desires. *Yes, you too can create whatever you want in your life! Just practice this simple technique*—which almost always turns out to be some variation on the power of positive thinking. *Picture in your mind what you want. Do it every day. Write it down.*

Infuse it with light. It will happen! And lo and behold, it does work—sometimes. Other times, not so well. But even when these techniques do work, the result is never abiding happiness. It's like a game of whack-a-mole: achieve one desire and another pops up to replace it. The truth is, *we don't know what we want.* Not really. None of us do. We can't. According to the Course, we're incapable of it—because we believe we are something we're not.

Neither fortune nor fame, health or longevity, success or romance, adventure or security, will guarantee happiness. Sure, for a time, any one of these might bring a grin to your face and a spring to your step. But only for a while. Success soon fades and becomes "the new normal" out of which some other goal will rise up and call to you, promising to restore to you the joy you once felt. Happiness that rests on external circumstances is too easily dashed upon the rocks of sudden tragedy: an unexpected death, a job setback, the discovery of infidelity. And even if you are blessed with good luck beyond measure, it's pretty much guaranteed that you will grow old. And you will die. That much is certain. Worse, so will every single person you know and love.

A bleak picture, no doubt. But is that all there is, my friends? Is that our inevitable fate? Or might there be an alternative? Why should happiness be so fleeting, so difficult to attain and impossible to hang on to?

Searching for Happiness, Finding Truth

The eighteenth-century German poet and all-around genius, Johann Wolfgang von Goethe, grappled with this problem in his monumental work *Faust*. It tells the tale of an unhappy doctor—world-weary and depressed—who seeks fulfillment but cannot find it. He makes a bargain, or bet, with the devil, Mephistopheles, in which Faust will give up his soul if Mephistopheles can bring to him an experience so profound and meaningful that Faust will wish for that moment to endure forever. In others words, Faust seeks to transform the ephemeral into the eternal. The devil proceeds to woo him with power, magic, women, wine, and beauty, but however compelling, none of these do the trick. There is nothing the devil can offer within the world of time that can make time stop and open the door to eternity. Only when Faust discovers the joy of helping others does he wish the moment to stay—but at that point he's already arrived at divine truth and, as a result, his soul is no longer in peril. God and His angels step in to thwart Mephistopheles and lift Faust into heaven.

In a more mundane but more nuanced setting, French author Marcel Proust, in his seven-volume *Remembrance of Things Past* (À *la recherche du temps perdu)*, describes in beautiful, exacting detail his protagonist's failed journey to capture happiness through romance or social status. Even so, sprinkled throughout the novels are moments when some otherwise insignificant sensory cue sets him free from the bonds of time and allows him to enter a timeless reality, a moment in which fear of death disappears. (I will have more to say about this sort of experience in chapter 3.) The search for happiness within the world, as the world defines it, is a losing proposition. However, there is a greater reality and it is always present—if we have the eyes to see and ears to hear. When we encounter such moments, the trivial opens into the transcendent, where happiness is a given.

Long before Proust and Goethe, another man grappled with the fragile, elusive nature of happiness, but working at it from the opposite direction. Siddhartha Gautama was a prince living in the sixth century BCE in what is today the country of Nepal. Siddhartha had the ideal life: amazing parents (the king and queen); kind and loyal courtiers; a comfortable palace with gorgeous, walled-off grounds; a beautiful, loving wife and bright, healthy children. His life brimmed over with happiness. He lacked for nothing. But one day he decided to venture beyond the protected palace grounds. He had been warned not to go out there, but his curiosity would not let him rest content in his sheltered life. He had to know more. What Prince Siddhartha encountered that day beyond the palace walls changed his life forever, along with the lives of millions of others down through the ages. It planted the seed for what would later become his awakening into enlightenment. It inspired the core of the teachings that today we recognize as Buddhism.

What did Prince Siddhartha see when he left the paradise that was his home? He beheld a sick man, an old man, and a corpse. He confronted the reality of illness, aging, and death. Having witnessed this, he could no longer remain in his beautiful Eden-like palace, because he knew it was a lie. And so he left forever, abandoning parents, wife, children, and all the perks of royalty for a spiritual quest to find a better way. After many failed attempts, he found that better way and attained enlightenment, seated in meditation under the *bodhi* tree. No longer Siddhartha, he dropped his personal identity to become the eternal Buddha.

At the heart of the Buddha's teachings lie the Four Noble Truths. We will only concern ourselves with the first two, as they directly address the problem of happiness that does not last. The First Noble Truth proclaims that all life is *dukkha*, that is, dissatisfaction or suffering. The second tells us that such dissatisfaction and suffering arise from thirst: an inner emptiness that drives us to chase after certain objects, people and outcomes in a futile attempt to quench that thirst. Abiding happiness cannot be found within the world as we know it. In our desperate attempts to secure it, we are like parched, shipwrecked sailors who guzzle seawater to slake their thirsts. The salt in the water dehydrates them, and instead of quenching their thirst, makes it all the more intense. In the same way, each object, person, or experience we pursue as the key to our missing happiness serves only to increase our thirst and intensify our longing.

The Truth Is You

A Course in Miracles is in total alignment with the Buddha's first two Noble Truths. It tells us that, left to our own devices, we will not find lasting peace, love or happiness. The reason? We're looking for love in all the wrong places. We're slaking our thirst with seawater. Worse yet, we don't know where, or *how,* to find pure water. Does it even exist, or is it just a fantasy, a myth? But there's an even more fundamental problem, and it lies at the root of the others. *We don't know who we are.* Yep, that's correct. We're going about the pursuit of happiness all wrong because we don't understand our true nature. We've been hoodwinked into believing that we are sea creatures and that saltwater is good for us.

Another way to think of this is, we're unknowing victims of identity theft. Until we recover our true identity from the interloper who stole it (the *ego*, according to the Course), the search for happiness, love, peace, and satisfaction will prove fruitless. Happiness must come from truth; otherwise it's delusional. And, *The X-Files'* Agent Mulder to the contrary, the truth is *not* "out there" waiting for us just around the bend. Truth resides within.

You can't get to truth if you start from false premises. If you're convinced that two plus two equals five (because your father told you so, or some professor or politician, or your latest "friend" just posted it on Facebook), then all subsequent calculations will be flawed. If an eagle seeks happiness in the belief that it's an ostrich, it will never spread its wings and soar; it will scamper about, clawing frantically at the ground, seeking the best hole in which to stick its head. And no hole will satisfy it. A cat will never achieve happiness chasing cars and gnawing on bones.

To find happiness, we must first undo the barriers to recognizing our true identity, which, according to *A Course in Miracles*, is Spirit. Collectively, we are God's offspring, God's Child, God's Son, created in the likeness of our Creator. But here too our identity confusion befuddles us. We picture God in *our* image: as a body, traditionally male, clothed in white, peering down on us from heaven and making judgments about who will live and who will die, who will thrive and who will suffer, all based on whether they've been nice or naughty. That's not God; that's Santa Claus. It's certainly not the God of *A Course in Miracles*.

Instead, try to think of God as a vast, infinite, unified field of perfect love—and nothing else. (Equivalent terms would be joy or bliss; in Sanskrit, *ananda*.) Since very few humans have ever experienced such love, it's almost impossible to imagine. But if God is perfect love, and God created us "in His image," then we must also be perfect love. Our true nature is not the body we see reflected in the mirror, nor the separate and private mind that's housed within that body. If we believe that's all we are and search for happiness on that basis, it will elude us again and again. Only when we recognize and remove the obstacles to our true nature—to love's presence within us and our fellow beings—will we know the truth of who we are. And as the Gospels tell us, the truth will set you free. Nothing else will do it.

The goal of this book is to get you started down the path to truth. But *A Course in Miracles* will carry you much farther—as far as you're willing to allow. The Course is designed to bring you to an experience of Spirit, of miracles, of oneness, and of your true Self, which is no different than God—that vast, eternal energy field of purest Love. Without such experience, we remain imprisoned, no matter how many books we read or workshops we attend. But having had that experience, even once, we *know* with total conviction what is reality and what is not, what is worth striving for and what is not worth our slightest effort. When we fall back into fear, guilt, or anger, we will understand the reason why. We can find our way out again.

The path is both simpler than you might think and at the same time ridiculously difficult. Simple, because it's the truth, and what could be more straightforward than to let truth be itself? But difficult, because all of our customary learning and experience lead us in the opposite direction. Without real commitment, our old habits of mind continue to dominate and resist change. They cling to us and slow us down, like trying to slog through thick mud in heavy boots. In the pages that follow, you will find a way through the mud. I'm rooting for you. We all are because, as *A Course in Miracles* makes clear, we walk that path together, or not at all.

Consider this book a toolbox to help you escape from the false identity that holds you captive. Consider it a beacon to see you through the darkness of this world—its false promises, shadowy misperceptions, and empty temptations—and light your way to freedom. Consider it a series of arguments designed to assist you in shuffling off the heavy garment of the false ego self that has so bedazzled you with its illusions and conned you into believing that *it* is actually *you*. When you do so, you'll find that the outcome is not some existential crisis. You are neither meaningless nor alone. No, the outcome is nothing less than joy: unconditional, abiding joy that is not of this world, but which you will recognize and welcome more surely than anything you've ever known in your life.

1

You Are What You Seek; You Seek What You Are

No one but yearns for freedom and tries to find it. Yet he will seek for it where he believes it is and can be found.[1]

For what could more surely guarantee that you will not find salvation than to channelize all your efforts in searching for it where it is not?[2]

A woman walks down a street at night. She spies an older man down on his hands and knees, frantically pawing at the ground in the halo of a streetlight. Assuming he's ill, she stops and asks what's wrong. He replies that he's lost his car keys and can't get home without them. He's desperate to locate them. She rapidly scans the cone of light around the streetlamp and sees at once that there are no keys lying there. Sensing that the man may be drunk, or perhaps a bit crazy, she asks where he might have lost his keys. He gives a vague wave in the direction of the darkened street and replies, "Somewhere over there maybe? I'm not sure." "Then why," she asks, "are you searching for them here?" He looks up at her as if she's the crazy one. "Because it's dark over there. I can't see."

When you begin searching for something important, the key question is: where do you look? Look in the wrong place—however familiar or convenient—and you're guaranteed not to find what you seek. This applies whether you're searching for your keys, your reading glasses, sunken treasure, or eternal truth. If you get thrown off by bad advice, misleading clues, or a poorly drawn treasure map, your search is doomed. You'll grow frustrated. Eventually you'll give up, concluding that whatever it is you were seeking is impossible to find, or more likely, that it does not exist and probably never did. You've learned from hard experience that anyone making that same search must be a fool.

The sad thing is that, once you've reached this point, you could walk right by your treasure and never know it. It could stride up and shout "Boo!" right in your face, and you'd turn away with a dumb grin and keep right on walking. So if we're searching for truth—in this case, the truth of who and what we are—then where do we start looking?

Streetlights to Nowhere

There are three time-honored streetlights under which those who seek truth begin their search. They are science, religion, and philosophy. Science attempts to find truth through experimentation, religion through faith, and philosophy through reason. Like the joke about the three blindfolded wise men who try to describe an elephant, one by feeling its trunk, another its torso, and the third its leg, so do science, religion, and philosophy each get some things right, yet still manage to miss the big picture. Let's briefly look around in the light shed by each to see what we find.

SCIENCE

The scientific method involves proposing a theory about how things work and then proving or disproving it through experimentation. The scope of any particular experiment is narrow, however, yielding one meager result, one slim slice of truth at a time, instead of the big picture. The idea is that all the little slices can someday be collected and assembled, and eventually they will add up to truth. But this is not necessarily the case. As with the elephant, the whole turns out to be more than the sum of its parts. And no single part is sufficient in and of itself to reveal the nature of the whole.

Furthermore, experimental results are subject to revision when new findings disprove the old and overturn the status quo. Medicine is a case in point. In the 1960s, for example, gastric ulcers were thought to be caused by stress that led to excess stomach acid production. In the 1980s it was discovered that in fact they were caused by the bacterium *H. pylori*. Likewise, until recently few questioned the theory that arteriosclerotic heart disease was due to high levels of cholesterol that built up in messy plaque along the arterial walls. Only lately have studies suggested the far more significant role played by inflammation.

But there is a still greater problem with scientific experimentation as a path to truth. Researchers are hampered by (1) the tools available to them (even the most brilliant and determined scientist could not have known about bacteria until the invention of the microscope); and (2) by their level of understanding. If their understanding is in any way inaccurate or prejudiced, then so too will be their results.

There's a joke that beautifully illustrates this dilemma. An amateur scientist sets out to sea to determine the precise range of sizes of the fish that live off the coast. He idles his boat twenty miles offshore and lowers his nets into the murky waters repeatedly, each time carefully measuring the lengths of the different fish trapped inside. After he's run his experiment a dozen times or more, he feels confident in boldly stating that the ocean contains no fish smaller than three inches in length. His mistake? His nets were woven with a three-inch mesh—that is, the spaces between the strands of netting were three inches apart. Smaller fish slipped right through the holes, unnoticed by the scientist, who had failed to consider the limits of his equipment when drawing his conclusions.

Science weaves many "nets" that it casts out upon the world, each one a hypothesis about the way things work. Depending on the "catch"—the results of experimentation—the hypothesis is either proved or disproved. But those nets do contain holes. The "holes" are the assumptions unconsciously built into the hypothesis, yet not recognized as part of it. The most glaring of these is the idea that the world is objective, external to the self, and fully real in its own right; that it exists independently of the mind. Therefore, the experiment is independent of the mind of the experimenter. One does not influence the other. Quantum mechanics has already raised serious questions about this notion. Given the nature of such assumptions, it is doubtful that science will ever be able to arrive at the truth.

At some distant future time, perhaps, with perfect instruments and impeccable theories, science could come very close to elucidating absolute truth. Yet even then, that truth could be overturned by the next experimental result. Science is always subject to revision, whereas truth, by definition, is certain. It does not change. Therefore science is not a viable path for seeking truth. Truth remains true, independent of experimental outcomes and their inherent biases.

RELIGION

What is the purpose of religion, if not to reveal the truth? Once we know that truth, all else should become clear: how to live properly, how to treat our fellow humans and the earth. But different religions understand truth in different ways. As a result, like the scientists, each searches for it in terms that align with its core assumptions and beliefs. In other words, each religion looks for truth within the radiant halo of its own special streetlight. Dare to search under a different streetlight, or worse, by bringing your own flashlight, and you are judged a heretic.

A learned professor of religious studies once taught me that the main difference between the Western religions of Judaism, Christianity, and Islam and the Eastern religions of Hinduism, Taoism, and Buddhism lay in the fundamental question they were attempting to answer. For the West, that question is: *what is the world?*

The Judeo-Christian tradition presupposes the reality of the outside world and then attempts to find the proper role of the individual within that world. At the very start of Genesis, God creates the heavens and the earth, the animal kingdom, and pretty much everything else before turning on the sixth day to the creation of human beings in the person of Adam. The world predates humankind. We are the last ones to the party—born into a world already established and sanctioned by God Himself.

For the Bible, then, the external world is real and absolute. How an individual behaves within that world is what matters to God. Therefore the body and its deeds take primacy over the inner workings of mind and thought. Indeed, the entire Hebrew Bible reads as a history of the world (unless one interprets it as parable, as I do with Exodus in my book *From Plagues to Miracles*).

However, the idea that the external world is fully real and that God created everything in it runs into trouble right away in the form of the problem of evil (also known as theodicy). There is evil in this world; that is indisputable. Humans can be very cruel to each other. Did God create this evil? If not, then how could it exist? If so, then what kind of God would do such a thing? And for what purpose? To "solve" the problem of evil, theologians had to add in another force that opposes God: namely, the devil. But this only complicates the picture and leads to more questions. Did God create the devil too? Can a God of love and goodness create a being committed to opposing love and goodness? And if God did *not* create the devil, then how could he exist in the first place, unless he is equal to God in status—another First Cause? But if this this were the case, then God would no longer be all-powerful. God would no longer be God.

These difficult questions lead rapidly into the tangled brambles of theology, with no satisfactory way out: no answers other than faith. As for the more practical question of how to achieve lasting peace and happiness, Western religion offers a system of rules for how to behave. Yet these necessarily vary from culture to culture and era to era. Shellfish are forbidden in the Hebrew Bible, but it's permissible to sell a daughter into slavery. For all of these reasons, Western religions fail to offer a viable path to truth.

The Eastern religions start from a different premise. They don't focus on the question *what is the world?* Consequently, they never make the assumption that the external world is real and therefore a creation of God. Instead, they ask: *what is the self?* Through meditative inquiry, the seeker arrives at an understanding that if anything can be called real, it is the mind and only the mind. The external world is understood to be a by-product of mind—a dream into which we somehow stumbled and lost our way, and from which we need only to awaken. This is also the position taken by *A Course in Miracles,* as we'll discuss in the next section.

According to this understanding, evil is simply another by-product of mind, no different from any other phenomenon. God did not create it for some mysterious hidden purpose that lies beyond our ability to comprehend. Nor is there any need for a devil. We are free to undertake our own inner inquiry as to what is real. And when we do, the only certainty we arrive at is that awareness—consciousness—exists. This parallels somewhat the philosopher René Descartes' famous dictum *cogito ergo sum*: *I think, therefore I am*. But a more accurate rendition would be: *awareness is, and that is what you are.*

PHILOSOPHY

The inadequacies of science and religion leave us with philosophy as our only remaining path to truth. And here the news is both good and bad. Philosophy lives in the realm of highly abstract ideas, which is not necessarily a bad thing. But philosophical arguments are difficult to follow and are detached from ordinary life experience. We tend to dismiss them as irrelevant. Philosophy does strive for internal consistency. In this regard, at least, it is congruent with truth. But the answers it offers to the big questions lack science's applicability and its standards of proof. Nor can they match religion's raw emotional wattage and its potential for transcendent experience. Philosophy rarely changes hearts or transforms minds.

A Course in Miracles is philosophical in its reasoning, its fondness for abstraction, and its absolute commitment to truth. It is scientific (or at any rate empirical) in that it asks us not to take what it says on faith, but to apply its principles directly to our lives and observe the outcome. And while it is not a religion—involving neither leaders, churches, nor a set of laws—it is spiritual because it focuses unswervingly on the transcendent—that which lies beyond the world of the senses. The Course is all about God—but not the God taught in Sunday school. The God of *A Course in Miracles* is identical with truth and love.

This is not the omnipotent overlord, prone to angry outbursts, who fashioned humankind from a lump of clay, who can read your every thought and knows your every deed, and who sits in judgment over you. The Course's God does not exist outside of you, in some heaven above, but deep within your own mind. As we noted in the Introduction, God did indeed create you, but as spirit—mind—not a body. Nor is God responsible for anything that happens to you in the outside world. According to the Course, God is unaware of the world, because it is our invention, not His creation. To find truth, you must look, not outward to the world, but inward, to God.

Become as Little Children

The quest for truth can take many paths. Moses climbed to the top of Mount Sinai to encounter God firsthand. Muhammad entered a cave to pray to Allah. Jesus went into the desert wilderness. Buddha sat in meditation under the branches of the bodhi tree. When we seek truth sincerely, we will find it, sometimes in the strangest of places.

Children's stories are an overlooked repository of truth. Take for example the well-known nursery rhyme:

Row, row, row your boat,
Gently down the stream.
Merrily, merrily, merrily, merrily,
Life is but a dream.

Here we find a set of guidelines for living a meaningful spiritual life. Be sure to row, row, row—that is, to show up and put in the effort, many times if necessary—but to do so gently, and always flowing with the current, not paddling against it. Do this joyously, merrily. The word "merrily" is repeated four times, the word "row" only three, emphasizing the relative importance of each. And then the coda, the determining reason for this guidance: "Life is but a dream"—a truth that both Eastern religion and *A Course in Miracles* would heartily endorse.

Along similar lines, there is a simple children's book—a perennial favorite that I read to my kids when they were young—that depicts the search for spiritual truth in an unusually perceptive and direct manner. *Are You My Mother?* by P.D. Eastman tells the story of a baby bird who hatches and tumbles from its nest while its mother is off gathering food for it. Not knowing what its mother looks like, the baby bird wanders the world in search of her, bumping up against a variety of different animals and objects along the way (including a dog, cow, boat, airplane, and a bulldozer) and asking each one the only question that matters to it: "Are you my mother?" Each answers, "No," except for the bulldozer, which says, "Snort!" and then, in a surprising move, lifts the baby bird back to its nest, where it is finally reunited with its real mother.

You might wonder how this story qualifies as a spiritual classic. Let me explain. The baby bird sustains a terrible loss when it tumbles from the warmth and safety of its mother's nest to find itself all alone in a world it does not understand. Like Adam and Eve, it has suffered a fall—

only literally, and through no fault of its own. The search for its mother is about reunion and the return home. It would have obvious appeal to a young child, for whom fear of separation from its parent looms large. But it's not only children who experience such fear and to whom this story appeals. Indeed, substitute your generic spiritual seeker for the baby bird and you might find her wandering the world from Italy to India, Bali to Belize, asking various masters, "Are you my guru? Are you my teacher? Are you my path home?" Unlike the spiritual seeker, however, the bird receives a clear and immediate "no" and can get on with its search without wasting years in the process.

The same theme of losing our way and the journey home shows up, as we noted, in the story of Adam and Eve in Genesis, but also in the book of Exodus (lost and enslaved in Egypt, then searching for the Promised Land), Homer's *Odyssey*, *Parsifal*, Shakespeare's *The Tempest*, and countless movies and other works of classic literature. It's also the central premise of *A Course in Miracles*.

According to the Course, the biblical story of Adam and Eve is a metaphoric portrayal of our separation from God. Somehow, amidst the infinitude of love that is God and His Creation, an impossible split occurred in which we found ourselves seemingly separated from God, alone and lost in a strange, forbidding world that is unsafe, unloving, and a far cry from our original home in the eternal oneness of God.

Another way of understanding this is that we have fallen asleep and dreamed a very bad dream, a true nightmare of separation and loss, from which we cannot now remember how to awaken. And being lost in dreaming, we've forgotten that there's any alternative. The dream has become reality: all that we know. "*The Bible says that a deep sleep fell upon Adam, and nowhere is there reference to his waking up.*"[3] The quest for truth and the desire to return to our true home in love becomes so fundamental to our experience here that it drives our every action, even if we're not aware of it. We seek love everywhere, and when we do not find it, or it vanishes from our grasp, we settle instead for power, adulation, and riches.

But let's go back to *Are You My Mother?* The baby bird's loss and its search for its mother are but the uppermost layer of the story's meaning. Yes, we want to find our way home, back into the loving arms of the eternal Mother. We desperately crave that security and sense of belonging. We try to recreate it through relationships, family and community. But there is another, deeper motivation for the bird's search, and for ours as well. Because if the baby bird cannot find and identify its own mother, then it remains ignorant of its true nature. It does not know itself. It could just as easily be a dog or cow or bulldozer. The moment it identifies its mother, however, it also knows itself. It is a bird. It has wings. It can fly!

The goal of the curriculum, regardless of the teacher you choose, is "Know thyself." There is nothing else to seek.[4]

A Course in Miracles states that all conflict and confusion in this world are ultimately the result of not knowing what we are—of forgetting, or intentionally diverting our minds and blocking it out. "*This is a course in how to know your-self.*"⁵ The moment we remember our true Self (capitalized here because it is so much more than what we think of as self), all our seeming problems are resolved, because they all stem from this one source.

Achieving this is not as difficult as it might sound, fortunately, because that Self has never left us. It has simply been obscured, overwritten by a dramatic narrative of personal selfhood—our life story—that keeps us so preoccupied we no longer recognize our true nature. To use an analogy from the Course, the truth of our being is like a "forgotten song,"⁶ whose melody we hear only rarely and faintly, as if from a great distance, and never more than a few notes at a time, but which kindles in us the memory of a place so beautiful, a time so tranquil and welcoming, that we yearn to return there more than anything this world has to offer.

Remembering this song of Self is easy because it's reality: the only reality. It's always there, always waiting. At the same time, remembering is very difficult. Our minds drown out this forgotten song with raucous noise blared from multiple channels at high volume. Only rarely do they fall silent, allowing the forgotten melody to drift through. But because we wrote, performed, and recorded this raucous music, because it is the creation of our mind, we are very reluctant to turn down the volume, much less turn it off altogether. As a result, the forgotten song of Self goes unheard. We remain ignorant of what we are, ever searching, never finding.

The very fact that we don't know, according to the Course, is proof that we are deluded. "*Uncertainty about what you must be is self-deception on a scale so vast, its magnitude can hardly be conceived.*"[7] The part of us that must ask, "What am I?" cannot be the true Self, or it would have no need to ask. It would know. The Course calls this ignorant, separated part of the mind the *ego*, but it also deserves the name *Never-Mind*, because it is the part of the mind that can *never* know what it is, that can *never* find truth, and that *never* really existed in the first place. And in response to our deepest desire to remember our Self and return to the peaceful nest from which we tumbled, it responds consistently, "Never mind! You have more important things to worry about."

The spiritual search then is really an exploration of identity. It is an *inner* journey that asks *who am I?* or, more accurately, *what am I?*

> *There is no doubt that is not rooted here. There is no question but reflects this one. There is no conflict that does not entail the single, simple question, "What am I?"*[8]

This becomes the fundamental question we must address if we are ever to find happiness and peace. When we can answer *this*, we *are* home, safe in the arms of the eternal Mother Whom we'd forgotten we'd lost; certain in Her guidance, from which we strayed; and free from conflict or confusion of any kind, because we know now what we are. We know our lineage. We know Self.

When we look deeply inward in search of our true nature, we will encounter many potential candidates. Under scrutiny, all will prove false. But that's OK. We need to call them out, shine a light on them, and expose them for what they are and are not, so that we can begin to disidentify with them. We need to ask, "Are you my self?" and receive a "no" answer in order to move on and discover the Self that's real. Because when we strip away all that's false, eventually what's left, what can't be dismissed, must be the truth. When we expose the attributes of Never-Mind as nothing—vaporous and without substance or value—we will find ourselves far along the path to the true Self, what I am calling *Ever-Mind*.

Notions of Self: "Who Are You?"

In ancient Greece, above the entrance to the temple of Apollo at Delphi, where aspirants came to consult the famed oracle and learn of their fates, an inscription proclaimed, *Know thyself*. The implication is that if you know yourself, you also know your fate. Character is destiny. Understand one and the other will inevitably follow. Like the baby bird in *Are You My Mother?*, we must know our true nature in order to know who we are and what we're capable of. If that bird believed itself to be a cow, it would graze fields and try to moo, without much success. It would never spread its wings and soar.

Another insightful children's book, *Stellaluna* by Janell Cannon, exactly describes this dilemma. A baby bat tumbles into a bird's nest and, not knowing its true nature, is raised by birds instead. The bat makes for a terrible bird. It dislikes the bugs its bird mother feeds it. It gets scolded for hanging upside down and for preferring night to day.

But once Stellaluna is discovered by a group of bats who remind her of her true identity, she finds that she makes a splendid bat.

What characteristics then do we regard as essential to *self*? If eating fruit, hanging upside down, and flying comfortably at night make Stellaluna a bat, what qualities make us who we are?

*   *   *

You're at a party. A stranger walks up and asks, "Who are you?" How do you reply? For most of us, it's with our name. "Hi, I'm Bob," I might answer, or in a professional setting, "Hi, I'm Dr. Rosenthal." We speak our name and that's our identity. But as Shakespeare's Juliet so perceptively asked Romeo, "What's in a name? That which we call a rose / By any other name would smell as sweet."[9]

Indeed, what *is* in a name? Not very much, if we examine it closely. A name may reveal something about our background, say an Irish or Asian or Jewish name, but it says very little about who we are. Most of us didn't even choose our own names. The name is merely a label that was slapped onto us at birth, like those name tags we affix to our chests at a conference. If a name really did reflect some aspect of our true identity, then all Bobs and all Dr. Rosenthals would have to have something in common. It's a bit like saying one is an American. The name applies equally to Texas oilmen, Hawaiian surfers, farmers from rural Iowa, and Manhattan hipsters. Which is to say, it tells us very little. Names serve well as identifiers for others. They say nothing about how we see or know ourselves, much less about our true nature, our most fundamental sense of be-ingness.

If you entered the Temple of Apollo believing that your name was sufficient for "knowing thyself," you probably would have been turned away. What else then, other than a name, defines your sense of self? The obvious answer is your physical body.

From the moment you're born, you're identified with your body. You learn how to interpret the messages of its senses (pain, comfort, good and bad smells) and how to control its movements. Your parents hold you up in front of a mirror and point, telling you that the body you see reflected there is *you*. This body has been your constant companion for your entire life—since before you can remember. There has never been a time when you did not prioritize its demands for food, sleep, and relief from tension.

Our bodies are unique in their appearance, abilities, and history. Are we tall or short, pretty or plain? One body can jump and dunk a basketball, another shoots baskets from a wheelchair. Our bodies bear the scars (quite literally) of our past. An old injury might not be obvious to others, but when it starts to ache again, we feel it!

We control the body. It belongs uniquely to us. We can't swap our body with those of other people (except in movies), nor do we confuse our body with anyone else's. So perhaps the body is as good an answer as any for the question: what am I?

But there are problems with this. For one thing, the body grows older and changes remarkably in the process. In a mere ten years, a cute little five-year-old becomes a lanky, acne-ridden teenager. And the body at age twenty looks and feels nothing like the way it does at seventy. Has your sense of self changed in parallel with the body's aging? My father, at age eighty-three, confided to me that, although he now had trouble walking and his memory wasn't what it used to be, he still *felt* like himself. His fundamental experience of selfness was unchanged. It remained constant within him, independent of his aging body.

Your body undergoes myriad changes outside the scope of your awareness as well. The cells in your body constantly regenerate. In the span of seven years, not one of them remains the same. Your body underwent a total makeover and yet, incredibly, it had no effect on your sense of self.

Furthermore, where exactly in the body would your self be located? No one would argue that a foot or elbow is the seat of the self. It's got to be somewhere in the head. Behind the eyes, most likely. And yet even with your eyes shut, you still know who you are. You still feel like *you*. And in dreams, with all external perception blocked off, you still picture yourself as your body. Yet can you localize where in that dream body your identity lies? I'll bet not.

The body acts as your interface with and agent in the outer world. (We'll deal with the reality of that world in the next chapter.) You smell a casserole cooking in the oven, feel the pangs of hunger, and serve yourself a portion. You see that your hair is messy and comb it. You receive input through the senses and you control the output. Or so it appears. But your body can also act without your conscious awareness. In fact it does so every second. Your heart beats, you breathe in and out, your eyelids blink, your stomach digests—all outside of your awareness or control.

More perplexingly, there are measures of brain activity (called *evoked potentials*) which are found in experiments to spike well before the subject reports any conscious awareness of an intention to act. Some part of us knows what we are going to do before we do! There are also reflexes that completely bypass awareness. Step on a thumbtack and your leg is already in motion, pulling back, well before you experience pain or decide it might be a good idea to lift your foot. Who or what is pulling back that foot? Is it you or your body? Which is the real *you*? If the body can act independently, can it be equivalent to the self?

Perhaps it would be easier, and more accurate, to think of the body not as home to the self, but more as a symbol, a marker for living out our life story. The body was present to witness it all, every tragedy and every triumph. Think of the piece that represents you while playing a game, like the car or hat in the game of Monopoly. It travels around the board, landing on different properties, buying some, owing money on others, growing richer or poorer in the process, all according to the roll of the dice. But the car or the hat is not *you*. Those pieces do serve a purpose for a short time. They allow you to situate yourself on the board and play a game that can grow quite intense for a time. But when the game is over, the pieces go back in the box, while *you* go on your way to other, more important things.

All in all, the body turns out to be a less than satisfactory choice for the location of self. What are our other options?

*   *   *

Most humans begin to talk at around two years of age. Some start earlier, others later. Albert Einstein didn't speak until he was five. But unless there is some serious impairment, it is safe to say that at some point in childhood, we become fluent in our native tongue. We speak well enough to be understood by others, and we can listen and make sense of what those others are saying.

The acquisition of language is a huge step in development, but it has a darker side. When we learn to assign words to the people and things around us, we accentuate the gap between us and them. A more fluid sense of reality, one that allowed us as infants to feel fused with our mothers, for example, crystallizes into a distinct sense of self and other, self and not-self. I know who I am and I know who you are—and you are not me. We can talk to each other, but our minds remain separate. We are two selves, not one.

This distinction between self and other is further fueled by the development of an inner voice or monologue which talks to us from inside our heads. And once it starts, it never shuts up. This inner voice most likely arises as a result of absorbing and parroting back what we hear from our parents and older siblings. But whatever its origins, it offers a running commentary on our experience that's interrupted only by sleep or coma (or deepest meditation). This voice gladly instructs us on how to react to the people and situations we encounter. It seems to have an opinion about everything.

The inner voice becomes identified with our sense of self. Who else could be talking to us so privately from inside our own head, where no one else can hear? Who else would be privy to our every thought and feeling? Who but the self?

Yet here too we run into problems. The inner voice does not make all of our decisions for us. As we saw earlier, many body functions operate outside our awareness, and are therefore independent of that voice. Nor does this inner voice have power over us. We can hear its words, yet still defy it. We can eat that second piece of cherry pie or have another glass of wine. We can *go with our gut*, a body-based metaphor for using our intuition to circumvent this voice. And although the voice can identify emotions and tell us why it thinks we're feeling them and what to do about them, it does not really experience emotion itself.

If emotions are part of the experience of self—and who could argue they are not?—then where do they come from? Emotions can be triggered by circumstances wholly unrelated to our lives (for example, a heart-wrenching movie), from thoughts (the thought of someone you love dying, even though they are in perfect health) and from memories. None have anything to do with the inner voice.

It also turns out that many of us have more than one inner voice. (Some psychologists would say we all do.) There are entire systems of psychotherapy, including Psychosynthesis, Gestalt, and Voice Dialogue, whose goal is to uncover these different voices in order to free us from their overbearing influence. The critic, the dreamer, the schemer, the victim, the perfectionist, the comic—all can exist simultaneously within us. They selectively take center stage to comment on our lives, usually in a way that's not very helpful. In the extreme case of dissociative identity disorder (or D.I.D., which we will return to in chapter 5), these different voices actually arise from different personalities cohabitating within the same mind. If the inner voice were really the sole, unique self, this would not be possible.

Are You What You Remember?

Thus far, we have ruled out the name, the body, and the inner voice in our search for the self. What candidates remain?

Each one of us has a life story that is absolutely unique, more so even than our bodies. No one else has lived what we've lived and no one ever will. So perhaps the life story is what best defines the self. In which case, our true identity would be the sum total of everything we've lived—the myriad of impressions we've stored in memory, loosely organized around a central thread of I-ness that runs continuously through them all.

Let's assume that someday in the future, your entire memory could be digitized and copied onto a massive storage drive, the way you might upload a favorite movie to the cloud today. Your upload would include not just the particular scenes you recall from your past, but the manner in which you think and emote, as well as your body's habitual reaction patterns. You could access the taste of birthday cake when you were five or that beer on your twenty-first birthday, your first sexual encounter, your first awareness of mortality. When you open that file and scan its voluminous contents, there is little doubt that this is *your self,* only without a body. Everything that's *you* is in there—your memories and fantasies, your sense of humor, your fears, your noblest deeds and most shameful secrets—all are contained in that single, massive data storage file. Any question you asked it about your life, it could answer. Who but *you* could manage that trick?

On the other hand, can a collection of memories, however detailed and comprehensive, be the equivalent of *self*? Would this digital storage drive really be *you*?

There's no denying that we are sculpted by our life experiences. The girlfriend who broke your heart, the horse who broke your leg, the spouse who broke his promise—all were formative. Each one helped shaped the self you are today. You no longer go out with crazy redheads. You shy away from horses too. But these are mere attributes, patterns of behavior, not identity. Something is still missing.

For one thing, our memory of the past is unreliable. It is not like a video camera recording what occurred second by second with perfect veracity. Memory is malleable; it can be altered by later circumstances. A child scolded emphatically by her mother and told there is no way her uncle would have touched her *like that* at Christmas is likely to believe it. Preserving her relationship with her mother is more important than what she actually remembers having happened. Likewise, if an overzealous police detective reviews mug shots with a witness and in the process repeatedly and forcefully asks her whether the face pictured in one particular mug shot was the culprit, she will tend to come around and agree with the detective's suggestion, even if her first response was a definite no. This is why eyewitness testimony, once the gold standard for evidence in criminal prosecutions, has become increasingly suspect at trial.

Another consideration when thinking about memory as the basis of self is the phenomenon known as state-dependent memory. When a particular incident is encoded into memory under the influence of a mood-altering substance like alcohol, it may not be recalled in normal waking consciousness. Only when that same substance is reintroduced will the memory return. It's as though the memory were locked away in a vault and the key that reopens it is an altered mental state linked to a specific substance.

State-dependent memory can affect something as simple as a drunk misplacing his house keys during a binge or a student using psychostimulant drugs to cram for an exam. After a few drinks, the drunk miraculously recalls where he left the keys, while the student can't recall half of what she'd memorized a day later. That information can only be retrieved if she takes another dose and reenters the hyperalert state induced by the drug.

Strong emotions can act like drugs in that they flood the body with chemical hormones. And like drugs, they can induce state-dependent memory. Events that terrify or enrage us can disappear from normal memory until retriggered by a similar emotional state. In fact, *anything* associated with such powerful traumatic events has the potential to reawaken state-dependent memory. I've worked with survivors of childhood abuse who were triggered into panic by cues as seemingly innocuous as firehouse sirens, dark closets, the reflection of the full moon on water, the sensation of tight boots, and remote wooded areas. Each was associated with an unremembered psychological horror. The return of these memories was not welcomed by my patients, understandably. They did not fit with the competent adult self-images they preferred to present to the world. So we may ask, which is closer to the true self: the traumatic childhood memory or the adult who holds the memory but doesn't consciously remember it?

We can ask this question even of normal, nontraumatic memories. We remember what we want to remember, whatever supports our current view of our self and the world, whether positive or negative. Memories that clash with that view are forgotten or conveniently explained away as aberrations. If, for example, it's important for you to believe that your mother was a saint, then memories of her rage will not be welcome. When the sense of self undergoes a shift, however, these overlooked memories can resurface, because they no longer challenge our self-concept. In fact they lend credence to a new sense of self. As a therapist, I've witnessed this firsthand.

Cleo's Memories

Cleo, a professional musician, had suffered for decades from panic and depression. She had relied on antidepressant medication to keep her functioning, to the extent that her medication had taken on an idealized, almost magical sense of meaning for her, rather like a lucky rabbit's foot. At the first hint of depressive symptoms, she'd call me to request a dose increase, and, as if by magic, she'd feel better, at least for a while. However, she lived in terror of the day when she would reach the maximum allowable dosage; then her meds would no longer work.

Although she had a strong genetic predisposition for depression, Cleo and I both felt it was important to explore other possible sources for her symptoms. We found these in her childhood belief that it was her job to keep her depressed mother happy by constantly being "on stage" and performing—which of course carried the risk that one day her performance might not live up to expectations, her mother would plunge back into depression, and it would be her fault. This led Cleo to feel that she was loved only for performing and not for her true self. As a musician she had to perform frequently, and she anticipated each performance with dread for weeks ahead of time. In their aftermath, she felt exhausted and would often succumb to depression.

Cleo also felt abandoned and unloved by her father. (Both parents were at this point deceased.) He was an aloof and angry doctor who'd served in Korea during the earliest years of her life and therefore didn't even meet her until she was almost two. Her father scared her. She'd witnessed his rages and his violence toward her younger siblings. At the same time, she craved his love and approval. Her father played piano and encouraged her to play too, but at the point where her talents outshone his, he grew sullen and competitive. To maintain any connection with him, Cleo could not let herself excel. As with her mother, she could never be genuine in his presence and simply let the music flow.

In a seminal psychotherapy session, I asked if she knew of any little girls who'd had happy and carefree relationships with their fathers, unlike her own. Yes, she had a friend whose daughter would playfully climb all over him when she was little. The two of them laughed a lot together, she recalled. I then asked if there were any other adult men from her childhood, other father figures, who did *not* inspire fear. She immediately remembered an uncle—a calm, unassuming man who would hold her on his lap in a manner that made her feel completely safe and loved. In fact she'd known this uncle before her father had returned from the war. In a sense, he was her first real father. Yet she'd forgotten all about him and his loving influence.

Memories like these led to others, including positive memories about her father himself—how they would sit side by side on the piano bench while she played the melody line to his chords. She could sense the happy smile on his face, how proud he was of her. She took this memory of her father, added her uncle into it (standing behind her), and left my office beaming with a sense of love and belonging previously unknown to her. She felt it had ushered in a true healing with her father.

When Cleo returned home after our session, she found a letter waiting for her from a dear old friend who lived far away. This friend had been cleaning out old emails and happened to discover one she'd gotten from Cleo some fifteen years earlier, six months before Cleo's father had died. In the email, Cleo recounted a concert performance and the typical anxiety she'd felt leading up to it.

The audience loved the concert. We sounded so good, I was really proud, and loved being in the spotlight. I felt like I belonged there: a real healing for the little girl who got terrified of all that applause. The most wonderful part was that my father sent me flowers that were presented to me at the end of the concert. We had spoken every night and I had told him about all the progress [I was making]. For the first time in my life, I felt I was sharing with a [real] father, one who was excited for his precious daughter. The night before the concert, he cried on the phone and told me to just keep my head up and that he knew I would be wonderful. I felt like something in me that was blocked started to flow . . . Such healing.

This unexpected window onto the past came to Cleo at the exact point where her image of herself and her relationship with her father had started to shift. She'd forgotten she had ever sent it, but now it served as confirmation of the changes already taking place within her. As her sense of self warmed and brightened, her past kept pace with it.

Cleo's story is yet another powerful demonstration that memory is fluid. It does not determine who we are. Just the opposite. Who we are—our self-concept—determines what we remember. Therefore memory cannot be equivalent to the self.

*   *   *

There is one final reason why the self is not simply the sum total of all past experience. We do not live in the past, when those experiences took place. Even when victims of trauma are triggered into flashbacks through state-dependent memory, reliving scenes of horror in their minds as if they were real and ongoing, they do not remain stuck there. Eventually, they emerge from the flashback and return to the present day.

The past is not where we experience our sense of self. The past is over. Gone. We live in an ongoing present. *Now* is the only reality, and therefore *now* is where we must seek for our true self as well. Search elsewhere, and you will come up empty-handed.

Clothing the Self: Values and Roles

We have auditioned a number of possibilities for the role of self and found them wanting. But we have not exhausted them all. There are more complex ways in which we construct our sense of self, ways we take for granted, barely noticing them until they're challenged. Enter the world of roles and values.

In the course of our lives, the roles we play out and the values we hold dear become the very scaffolding upon which our sense of self is built. We take pride in these. We hold fast to them, even unto death. Therefore, to fully understand who and what we are, we must expose these roles and values for the imprisoning chains they are. And then we must free ourselves from them.

Values and roles feed off each other. They intertwine. We acquire certain values from the roles we play, and we accept certain roles as a result of the values we hold. The whole topic is so complex that it could easily justify an entire book of its own. But for our purposes, we need only understand how these contribute to an image of self.

VALUES

Values form the backbone of the self-concept, because they determine how we behave and who we affiliate with. When we value a person, we will go out of our way to help them. If it's an idea we value, we'll defend it vigorously, even unto death, and we will feel a kinship with others who value the same idea. Communities were once defined around such common values, often of a religious nature, but also by shared goals or burdens. When the whole town attends the same church, gets a paycheck from the same factory, or turns out in a storm to pile sandbags against a rapidly rising river, those shared values will knit them tightly together.

Values vary markedly from one person to the next. For example, you and I may vote for the same political party and worship at the same synagogue, but have very different views about how to discipline children. In fact this inconsistency is the double-edged sword of values: we want to connect with those who share our values, but these same values divide us from those with conflicting beliefs. (We will look more closely at this phenomenon in chapter 4.) In extreme cases, opposing values become such a threat that anyone who subscribes to them is viewed as different, alien, inhuman even. This gives us the right to murder them—always in self-defense, of course—and yet we grow shocked and outraged should they dare to retaliate.

In every war, the enemy is depicted as alien: the *other*. They are called by pejorative names and racial slurs, which enable soldiers to psychologically distance themselves from the fact that they will be killing their fellow human beings. The enemy cannot be anything like us. They are inhuman monsters, trampling our values and intent on destroying our way of life and everything we love—unless we destroy them first. If, however, we happen to encounter the enemy face-to-face, in a personal context, they turn out to have far more in common with us than we'd imagined.

A powerful example of this occurred near the start of World War I in what is now known as the Christmas truce. German, French, and English troops were dug in, occupying deep trenches separated by a heavily barbed-wired stretch of land belonging to neither side and aptly dubbed no-man's-land. It was a kill zone; no one daring to enter survived. The lines of troops were a mere hundred yards apart, about the length of a U.S. football field—close enough to hear each other's conversations and smell each other's cooking. On Christmas Eve, 1914, in the midst of the fighting, peace broke out. Although no one knows for sure how the truce began, it seems the two sides were singing Christmas carols and both joined in the Latin hymn *Adeste Fideles*. This was followed by shouts of "Merry Christmas" and mutual promises of nonaggression: *we won't shoot if you don't*. The combatants exchanged gifts of cigarettes, food, and clothing. And both sides were finally able to bury their fallen comrades whose corpses lay decaying in no-man's-land.

The only ones unhappy with the truce were the generals, and, reportedly, a young German corporal by the name of Adolf Hitler, who decried the Germans' "lack of honor."

For the brief duration of this truce, the shared values of Christmas trumped patriotic duty and undercut the stereotypical image of the enemy. The German, French, and English troops were not so alien to each other after all. They shared a profound tradition in Christmas.

Of course, the truce did not last. Ultimately the more limited values that sparked the war prevailed, and the shooting resumed. By the time the war finally ended, it had claimed some fifteen million lives.

In today's world, largely because of the influence of social media and its ability to filter out opinions that differ from our own, values have become as entrenched as those World War I battle lines. We no longer bother to hear each other out. We don't *want* to. This increasing polarization masks the values we have in common, values that would humanize us to each other and allow collaboration to replace division. Republicans disdain Democrats and vice versa, often without bothering to learn about the value systems those labels represent. Are business and entrepreneurship really so at odds with help for the disadvantaged and stewardship of the environment? If we kept our minds open and ignored Facebook and Fox, we might find ourselves agreeing more often with those we thought we opposed. We would discover our common values. Who knows? Peace might one day break out again.

Examined honestly, a value is merely an opinion that we've elevated to the level of absolute, unwavering truth. Opinions can be questioned and changed when new information becomes available; not so with values. They become incorporated as part of the self. Therefore we will defend them blindly rather than change, even if it divides us from half the world. Even if it kills us all. How else to explain those willing to take life in service of an ideology, like a suicide bomber?

> *What you value you make part of you as you perceive your-self. All things [that] you seek . . . hide your worth from you, and add another bar across the door that leads to true awareness of your Self.*[10]

We may proudly and loudly proclaim that we love the causes we value, but the relationship is not one of love. It is enslavement. We allow these causes to control the way we see and act toward fellow humans. But make no mistake: in no way do values have anything to do with the true *Self*, any more than the clothes we wear or the TV shows we watch. Values can and do shift with age and experience. No value is absolute or universal. None will hold true in every circumstance. And there will always be those with different values to challenge yours.

ROLES

Life assigns us many roles to play. Some are forced on us; others we choose. The moment we're born, we enter a world of assumptions and expectations about who we will become and what we'll accomplish. These come primarily from parents, but also from siblings and the culture at large.

For most of human history, birth order and biological gender determined life roles. Males were breadwinners, dominant by force of strength and proneness to violence.

Females had fewer options, restricted by the demands of childbearing and child rearing. Fortunately, these rigid roles have started to change. Nevertheless, gender still largely determines how we're parented and taught about the world. Boys fight openly for dominance; girls strive to get along (while learning to manipulate behind the scenes).

In one experiment, adults of both genders were shown a brief video clip of a crying infant. When told that the baby was a girl, they responded with coos of sympathy. "Oh, she's so sad." When told he was a boy, the response was quite different. "Look at him! He's mad!" (In the next chapter, we will look at the role of context in how we perceive.) From our earliest days, we're taught that for boys anger is acceptable, even expected, while tears and sadness are natural for girls. Women who dare show anger are judged harshly. It doesn't comport with the conventional roles expected of them: mother and wife. The same holds true for men who cry when sad or admit fear. Such emotions have no place in the cold, competitive, dog-eat-dog worlds of business and warfare.

As children grow up, they take on additional roles determined by their personalities and abilities. Are you smart or slow, agile or clumsy, a leader or a follower, a risk taker or risk-averse, a loner or a people person? Do you delight in following the rules or breaking them? Each character trait pushes you toward certain roles and away from others.

Of course we can change roles we don't like. Adolescence and early adulthood are wonderful times to experiment and try on different roles. We rebel against what our parents foisted on us. We find new role models and try to emulate them. And as we mature, we may discover new abilities that went unrecognized by our families, abilities that allow us to play out other, higher-status roles.

Work and parenting add yet another layering of roles to this sense of self. A doctor is trained to be on call, to wake up and be available at all hours in an emergency, without overtime pay. A fireman puts life at risk to save others and witnesses death in forms that would make most of us sick—all a routine part of the job. A prostitute puts his or her body out there as a commodity, learning the moves by which we attract, and feigning intimacy for pay. I could go on and on with similar examples. In my book *From Plagues to Miracles*, I told the story of a man schooled by his father to become a white-collar criminal. The role filled him with pride at his ability to pull one over on his unwitting employer. But he also experienced shame because he knew it was wrong and had to hide what he did from everyone he knew, and because he lacked the education to change and find alternate gainful employment.

When you meet new people at a party, what you really want to know is not their names. It's who they are, that is, the roles they play and their values, and whether or not you hold any in common. Do they have kids? (That is, are mother or father among their primary roles?) Are their kids the same ages as yours? Are they good parents? (That is, do they share your parenting philosophy?) Are they single (potential partner material)? What do they do for work or career? (Is it higher or lower status than you?) Where did they grow up? Go to school? What are their interests, hobbies, political, and religious beliefs? (Can we get along and be friends?) These are the elements that make up identity in a social context. But are they *self*? If so, then we'd expect them to be a fixed part of us, unwavering right up to the moment of death. Clearly this is not the case. Every role we play will change or come to an end. Kids leave their parents; singles become couples; careers end in retirement, layoffs, or illness; friends and lovers break up, move apart, or eventually die.

In his wonderful book *Who Dies?* Buddhist writer Stephen Levine, who coached thousands of terminal patients through their dying process, asks us to consider what happens when illness and looming death strip us of our comfortable, familiar roles. When serious illness prevents you from working, who are you? When you are no longer able to drive a car and be independent, who are you then? When your legs fail and you can't walk, when control over your urine and bowels deserts you, who are you? Most extremely, when Alzheimer's robs you of memory so you no longer recognize the faces of your own children, who are you? In each of these circumstances, what is it that remains, and can it still be called *self*?

Clearly, trying to pinpoint the exact nature of the self is a slippery business. Values and roles may help us interrelate socially, but they cannot be said to define the self. If knowing who and what we are is essential to finding peace and happiness, then it's no wonder these elude us. We really don't have the slightest clue!

The Never-Mind

Like the baby bird in *Are You My Mother?*, we have now posed the question, "Are you my true self?" to many different candidates. It turned out that our names were not self. Our bodies also failed the test. So too did that insistent voice in our heads. Our memories and life story turned out to be too unreliable to serve as the bedrock on which the sense of self is erected. Besides, memory is rooted in the past, while the self exists in the present. And the cherished values and roles with which we embellish our identity will all eventually wear thin and fall away. None is adequate to describe our true self.

And yet each candidate did seem to capture something important about how we think of ourselves. Might we somehow combine them and cobble together a loose, working model of self? In fact, that combination is pretty much how most of us do view ourselves. We are the sum total of all that's happened to us in the past, represented on the game board of life by our physical body, directed by an inner voice, and shuffling multiple roles in concert with our own unique set of values. That's the sum total of our identity: our self-concept.

It seems to work, or at least to get us by. However, there are two serious problems with this particular self-concept. The Course tells us that truth, and therefore the true nature of self, is unchanging and unchangeable. (This makes sense. If it changed, then could it still be truth? Would the old version or the new one be more true?) Truth is forever itself. But as we have seen, the body, memory, values, roles—these do change. Therefore, no matter how we try to package them into a coherent sense of self, we can never arrive at anything that's stable, enduring, and true. On a more practical note, if this combination were in fact the sum total of who and what we are, then it has obviously failed at bringing us lasting happiness and peace. We might want to look for an alternative that offered better prospects.

In actuality, when we toss these various candidates for self together and stir, the concoction that emerges is not the true self. Nevertheless, it is one we strongly identify with. *A Course in Miracles* calls this false self the *ego*. I have called it *Never-Mind*. By whatever name, it poses the single greatest obstacle to finding truth, peace, freedom, and happiness. And it drives us to seek endlessly for these, forever fumbling around in the dim halo of a nonexistent streetlight.

> *"The concept of the self stands like a shield, a silent barricade before the truth, and hides it from your sight."*[11]

A Course in Miracles is very clear: the ego—the Never-Mind—must fail at reaching truth because it is itself untrue. *It does not exist.* When examined closely, its concept of self is revealed as naught but smoke and mirrors. It is a lie.

> *What is the ego? Nothingness, but in a form that seems like something. . . . There is no definition for a lie that serves to make it true.*[12]

How can nothingness satisfy? How can it achieve anything real, lasting, and substantial?

It is not possible to get to reality from unreality. You can't travel and get anywhere in a dream. You may think you're making progress, but it can all change or vanish in an instant, and now you find yourself back where you started, stuck in the same predicament. By definition, no illusion is true, ever; nor can the truth embrace illusions of any kind, in any way, yet still remain true. You can't allow a few little pathogenic bacteria in your drinking water and still call it pure.

Never-Mind is an impostor that has hijacked your true self and hidden it within a world of dizzying false choices and unresolvable conflicts: a world of clashing separate bodies, each shadow-boxing with its own reverie of the past; a world bound up in values and roles that distract you from the only purpose that would actually make a difference. It is a world in which inequality and suffering are tolerated, even venerated. And the Never-Mind has you convinced that *this is inevitable, this is your life*: a tiny blip amidst the random swirling chaos with little power to change anything and zero ability to survive. You see no way out—if you even bothered to look, which most of us do not. Never-Mind has assured us there is no point. As Shakespeare's Macbeth so beautifully describes it as his world comes tumbling down around him, "Life's but a walking shadow, a poor player / That struts and frets his hour upon the stage / And then is heard no more. It is a tale / Told by an idiot, full of sound and fury, / Signifying nothing."[13]

Fortunately, there is an alternative to this bleak picture.

Ever-Mind

It should be clear by now that if you seek truth, you must divest yourself of everything that's false. If it's happiness you desire, then you must root out all that breeds unhappiness.

If you want freedom, you must recognize the chains that bind you, no matter the form théy take, and pry them loose. And if you want peace, you must part ways with the part of you that thrives on conflict. To achieve truth, freedom, peace, and happiness, you don't need to take any specific action or formulate a plan. You don't have to *do* anything at all, because *doing* necessarily involves a physical body and a mind that regards itself as lacking in some essential quality that can only be obtained through action by a body. Action without direction leads in circles and gets you nowhere. You remain a prisoner of Never-Mind, running madly about within the confines of your self-created cell.

There is nothing to *do*, but a great deal to *undo*. You must tear apart the facade of self and knock down the barriers you've erected to recognizing truth. It can't be found in the past or in some imagined, idealized future. It's here, now, this moment. *This. Now. Moment.* And not anywhere outside of you either, because (as we'll see in the next chapter) there *is* nothing outside the mind.

> *Those who seek the light are merely covering their eyes. The light is in them now. Enlightenment is but a recognition, not a change at all.*[14]

Give up on the notion that somewhere there exists a special streetlight in whose resplendent glow you'll find the missing key to your joy, and that if you just keep searching, covering that same tired ground, one day you will find it. The light that shines the way to truth lives within you. Joy and peace are yours, not because of anything you do, but because of what you are: your true Self. *A Course in Miracles* calls this true Self which we all share the *Christ* or the *Son of God*. (Note how the Course gives these conventional Christian terms an entirely new and radically different meaning.) I will call this Self the Ever-Mind to contrast with Never-Mind, but also because it is forever and always itself: unchanging and unchangeable. It is Mind in its purest, abstract essence—nothing more, nothing less, because there *is* nothing else.

The essence of Ever-Mind is love—vast, blazing, unconditional love with no limits. Its attributes in this world are peace, joy, and freedom. Identify with Never-Mind, and these must elude you. Awaken to your reality as Ever-Mind, and they are yours without asking. It's all part of the same package.

In my book *From Plagues to Miracles*, I interpreted the characters of Moses and Pharaoh from the story of Exodus as symbols of Spirit and ego, or Ever-Mind and Never-Mind. I described the contrast between them in the following way:

> *[Ever-Mind] is not limited by time or space, or by the physical body. It doesn't fear for its survival, and therefore has no need to plan. It doesn't compare its lot with others. Where the ego [Never-Mind] yammers at us constantly, [Ever-Mind] understands silence. It guides, but never compels. It knows no guilt because it is incapable of doing harm. It operates through miracles, not forced action, and so the law of cause and effect does not apply to it. . . . Most of all, it brings with it a deep sense of peacefulness. The question or*

problem we struggled with isn't so much solved; it ceases to exist. Seen through the eyes of [Ever-Mind], there is no more question, no more problem. We simply misunderstood. And now, seeing clearly, our minds are at peace again.[15]

Here is one of many passages from *A Course in Miracles* that addresses the distinction between these two different versions of self.

The part of your mind in which truth abides is in constant communication with God, whether you are aware of it or not. It is the other part of your mind that functions in the world and obeys the world's laws. It is this part that is constantly distracted, disorganized and highly uncertain.

The part that is listening to the Voice for God is calm, always at rest and wholly certain. It is really the only part there is. The other part is a wild illusion, frantic and distraught, but without reality of any kind.[16]

We can use a computer analogy to better understand this distinction. Let's say that there are two different operating systems (OS) for the mind. OS1 is the Ever-Mind. It is, as its name implies, all about oneness or union. It is based in truth and exists independent of the outside world. When your mind runs OS1, everything you see and do falls into alignment and you are at peace. No matter how stormy and difficult the outer world appears to be, you abide in inner calm. Happiness is the natural and inevitable result.

A Course in Miracles calls OS1 *salvation* or the *Atonement*. You accept it into your life by making the decision to do so, and then allowing it to guide you in all your other decisions, because you recognize the futility of trying to decide them for yourself based on your old self-concept. Like the alcoholic in recovery with the help of Alcoholics Anonymous, you turn your life over to a higher power. The Course calls this higher power the *Holy Spirit*. It is the Holy Spirit Who is responsible for carrying out the plan of the Atonement. He directs its unfolding, including your particular part in it. When you learn how to accept the guidance of the Holy Spirit and allow Him to orchestrate your life for you, you receive true answers in the form of miracles.

The other operating system is OS2, the Never-Mind. As its name suggests, it arises from twoness, a false duality: the belief in a separate and uniquely individual sense of self that's split off from and fundamentally opposed to the oneness that is God and God's Son. Because OS2's programming is based on a set of false assumptions, the questions it asks and the answers it arrives at must also be false. A flawed operating system will give you flawed answers— every time. (Remember 2 + 2 = 5 from the introduction?)

"Ye shall know them by their fruits. . . . A good tree cannot bring forth evil fruit, neither can a corrupt tree bring forth good fruit" (Matthew 7:16, 18, King James Version).

Untruth cannot give rise to truth, nor truth to falsity. There are no exceptions.

God programmed OS1 when He created us in His likeness, that is, as an extension of Spirit and Ever-Mind. We made OS2 when we abandoned Ever-Mind and, in our fear and confusion, needed some way to try to make sense of what could never be understood: the ego and its world. Because only God is real, anything that thinks it is not of God, that thinks it is distinct and separate from God, must be unreal. Illusion. It does not exist in God's one reality. Therefore, OS2, the Never-Mind, is a fiction perpetrated on us by ourselves, a delusion we crafted and willfully wrapped ourselves in.

> *The self you made is not the Son of God. Therefore, this self does not exist at all. And anything it seems to do and think means nothing. It is neither bad nor good. It is unreal, and nothing more than that. . . . What power can this self you made possess, when it would contradict the Will of God?*[17]

In any given moment, you have a choice about which operating system you want to run. You do not lose this power of decision, because you cannot lose your true eternal nature. Even when slumbering deep within the dream of Never-Mind, the choice remains always available to you. You can run OS2 and live according to its flawed laws for years—your entire lifetime if you wish—and still, in the very next instant, change your mind—literally! According to *A Course in Miracles*, this is the only *real* choice of which you, or any of us, are capable: the only decision of any real consequence.

OS2 keeps you thirsty, confused about who and what you are, wandering and searching, but never finding, never satisfied. OS1 offers miracles: answers from the realm of truth that solve all seeming problems, because all problems spring from the same root: the false self, the ego. But as we shall see in chapter 6, what feels miraculous to the mind that runs OS2 is in fact perfectly natural to OS1. If you're accustomed to consistently getting wrong answers and navigating your life by them, then an answer that actually works will strike you as remarkable: a miracle.

The two operating systems are mutually exclusive; you can't run them simultaneously. You cannot serve two masters. Run OS1, and OS2 is no more. Choose OS2, and OS1 recedes . . . though as we said, it never disappears entirely. Illusions cannot displace truth.

> *The Holy Spirit, like the ego, is a decision. Together they constitute all the alternatives the mind can accept and obey. The Holy Spirit and the ego are the only choices open to you. God created one, and so you cannot eradicate it. You made the other, and so you can.*[18]

The OS you choose will determine your self-concept as well. Are you nothing but ego, the Never-Mind? Or are you Ever-Mind, the one eternal Child of God? You decide. In fact, that's *all* you get to decide. But from that one decision, everything else will follow.

2

Believing Is Seeing

Perception selects, and makes the world you see. It literally picks it out as the mind directs.[1]

What you desire you will see.[2]

My grandfather Arthur immigrated to the United States from Russia in 1922. He lived through the Bolshevik Revolution of 1917 and had many stories to share from that tumultuous time, including finding himself in front of a firing squad not once but twice and living to tell the tale. There was however one particular story, far less dramatic, that nonetheless made the greatest impression on me.

The Marxists came to power in 1917, intent on showing the Russian people that their new system of government was superior to the capitalism of the West. To this end, they publicly screened a short film clip that depicted just how miserable conditions were in the United States. In the film, a group of young men, undoubtedly starving, spied a loaf of bread on the ground and immediately began a mad chase for it. They ran hard, shoving one other out of the way in the attempt to reach that precious loaf of bread. So scarce was food in the United States that they dived and piled on top of each other, trying violently to wrench the bread away and tear off a small piece to ease their hunger. The film made an impression on my grandfather.

But he'd heard other, different rumors about the West, so he traveled through Europe, eventually boarding a steamer bound for the port of New York. He wanted to see the United States for himself firsthand. He'd assumed at the time that he'd return to Russia and his family, but he never had the chance. Most of his family perished in the Nazi concentration camps. (He tearfully confided to me that he'd never said a proper goodbye to his mother, thinking he'd be seeing her again.)

Once in the United States, he contacted relatives who helped him find work, and soon enough he had a little store of his own. With a few dollars of spending money in his pocket, my grandfather started frequenting the cinema. One day, sitting in the darkened theater before a Charlie Chaplin film, he burst into uncontrollable laughter. I can only imagine the looks on the faces of those seated around him, because the Chaplin film hadn't yet begun. The footage he found so hilarious was a sports reel, a clip from a football game, and as the players hustled downfield after a fumbled punt and piled atop each other trying to recover it, he realized that *this* was what he'd been shown in Russia. It was not a loaf of bread the men had chased; it was a football. They were not desperate or starving. It was a game! The Bolsheviks had taken footage from a sports reel and stripped it of all context in order to bolster their ideology and prove that communism was superior to capitalism. Waiting in long lines for bread in Russia was not easy, but it was much better than having literally to fight for it in America.

When it comes to perception—how we see the world—context is everything. Place an average-sized adult among NBA basketball players and she'll look puny. Stand her beside a kindergarten class and she's a towering giant. All perception depends on context. This holds true from the cellular level on up. Without context, we can't evaluate what we're seeing, hearing, or touching. We need *context* in order to provide *contrast*. Otherwise it is impossible to make the distinctions on which perception relies.

Photographers know that, if you want to convey the grandeur of an Alpine panorama, you must place a human figure somewhere within it. The tiny figure allows the viewer to gauge the enormity of the mountains surrounding it. We need both a center on which to focus and a background against which we contrast the center. In a word, we need context. Without it, perception loses meaning.

When Context Goes Missing

A number of years ago in my psychotherapy practice, a new patient informed me that he'd consulted with a colleague of mine, Dr. B., for two visits, but things didn't work out. I did not know Dr. B. personally, but she had a solid reputation in the professional community, so I was puzzled about why he'd felt he couldn't work with her. He explained that in their two sessions together, he had shared painful details from an abusive and shameful childhood sexual experience—the first time he'd confided this to another human being—and although she certainly tried to look and sound empathetic, she was obviously uncomfortable with what he'd related. She'd fidgeted and squirmed in her seat and at one point bolted upright to pace back and forth, turning her gaze away from this man to stare out the window. My patient concluded, quite understandably, that Dr. B. had her own unresolved issues with sexual abuse. How could he work with such a therapist? Try as I might, I couldn't disagree. Contrary to her reputation, clearly Dr. B. was not a competent therapist. She was impaired, at least in this one area.

But as a student of *A Course in Miracles*, I knew all too well the warning signs of ego at work. The intensity of my negative reaction to Dr. B.'s behavior clued me in. Therefore I made a conscious decision to release my judgments about her. I would not try to excuse her behavior to my patient, because that would be counterproductive. How many abused kids have been given nothing but excuses for why their abusers did the things they did? But in my own mind, I forgave Dr. B. for her failings. After all, who was I to judge her and whatever demons from the past she might be wrestling with? In my mind, I wished her well.

A short time later I was having lunch with another colleague and for some reason Dr. B.'s name came up. I held my tongue about what I'd heard from my patient and simply listened. I learned that Dr. B. was indeed having a hard time, but not in the way that my patient or I had imagined. Dr. B. had only recently undergone extensive back surgery, and it had not turned out well. She was in great discomfort much of the time, especially at her office, because she refused to take painkillers while seeing patients. She could only sit for brief intervals before the pain grew so intense that she had to move around.

Now I understood why Dr. B. had squirmed and paced about. Now I had the full context—and it had nothing to do with my patient's abuse memories, however difficult and unsavory they may have been to hear. No, Dr. B. was in physical pain. My only remaining question was why she had not shared this with the patient. I assumed she was trying to maintain a professional boundary, and how could I fault her for that?

What exactly happened here? My patient, operating within the powerful context of his sexual abuse and the shame he felt about it, assumed that everyone, including his therapist, would feel similarly. He focused in on a narrow band of information—Dr. B.'s obvious discomfort—as proof that his conjecture was correct. And striving to be empathetic to his point of view, I too assumed he was correct, to the point where I questioned the competence of a colleague. Both our perceptions were influenced by the contexts we brought to them from our pasts: for my patient, his abuse; for myself, the sad fact that over the years I'd encountered no small number of therapists attempting to heal their own wounds through their patients. But neither of us had all the relevant information—not by a long shot!

There is a clever video about the selective nature of perception that's been circulating on the Internet for years.[3] In it, we see a group of six people standing in a circle in a mid-sized room. Half wear white shirts, the other half black. We're instructed that they will be passing two basketballs back and forth between them, and our task is to pay close attention and accurately count the number of ball passes made by the players in white. At the end, we'll learn how well we did.

As we stare fixedly at the ball and count passes only among the white shirts—one, two, three—someone wearing a gorilla suit walks through the middle of the room, right through the circle, even pausing to stare at the camera and beat his chest—but most of us don't even notice! We're too intent on those ball passes, overly focused on what we were told to pay attention to, and therefore missing completely what we weren't looking for, even though it was quite striking and, under normal circumstances, impossible to miss.

In this instance, we intentionally stripped away context, because all we cared about was following that ball and getting the count right. We decided in advance what was important (based on what we were told) and therefore missed the big picture.

Magicians use sleight of hand in the same way to direct our eyes away from their covert manipulations. They mask the full context of what they're doing from us, and we willingly play along, because we want to enjoy the surprise reveal at the end of the magic trick. Politicians use a similar bait-and-switch tactic to avoid addressing difficult issues for which they have no real solutions and instead focus their voters' attention on simplistic slogans.

The conscious manipulation of perception through misdirection and narrowing of context isn't confined to magicians, politicians, and men in gorilla suits. We use it ourselves all the time. We become so intent on finding a romantic partner, for instance, that we intentionally overlook warning signs of jealousy, alcoholism, or road rage. We brush these aside, minimizing them in order to focus narrowly on our love interest's positive qualities. But with time and repeated incidents, it becomes ever more difficult to maintain the fiction. The larger context breaks through, and we break up.

Con men (and women) become adept at manipulating context in order to bilk their marks out of millions. They dangle the prospect of windfall returns, promising that whatever scheme they're peddling is a surefire win and that the victim should just ignore all those envious naysayers. To get in on the deal, all that's needed is some cash up front. The gullible marks become so convinced, so attached to the certainty of easy riches, that they refuse to consider any evidence to the contrary. One notorious huckster was arrested just as he was about to close a con. When the police informed his mark that he'd been the victim of a confidence man, they were surprised by his reaction. He was not grateful, as might be expected. He was furious, believing they'd screwed up the deal of a lifetime for him.

We can marvel at such pigheadedness, but we are all guilty of the same sort of behavior. We are all victims of a con perpetrated by Never-Mind. It tantalizes us with its promises of happiness in the form of love, fame, riches, and power. When these fail, and it is exposed for the fraud it is, instead of feeling relief, we get angry. We persist in the con. *I refuse to believe he'd cheat on me; he just told me he loved me. That stock will come back, I'm certain of it. My next music video will go viral on YouTube, making me famous and rich.*

The Pitfalls of Perception

The proclivity to ignore context and focus instead on what we want to see is rooted deeply in the way our senses operate. Eyes must focus if they are to see; ears must mask out superfluous sound if they are to hear. Perception must select one figure from the background, one signal from amidst the noise. It's not possible to take it all in simultaneously and have it make sense. Even if the physical eye registers light and the ear hears sound, it still requires experience to understand *what* is being seen and heard, that is, to distinguish foreground from background, central from peripheral, object from setting, and to make meaning of it all.

Congenital cataracts (that is, cataracts present at birth) were one of the main causes of blindness until reliable surgical procedures were devised to remove them. Doctors fully expected that, once removed, the blindness would be instantly cured and patients would for the first time in their lives gain full vision. Much to the surgeons' surprise, however, these patients did not see—not at first. Yes, their eyes "saw" something out there, but only vague shapes and colors without context or meaning. Only with time did they learn to interpret shapes and colors and refine their vision to what we would consider normal.

Similarly, members of indigenous tribes who have never seen a television are unable to discern images on the screen as we do. Their brains have never learned to organize the thousands of pixels (or their digital equivalents) into recognizable, meaningful forms. Only with repeated exposure to and interaction with the environment do the senses mature and fine-tune themselves.

When we think about this, it really shouldn't be surprising. Our senses themselves operate a bit like the pixels on a TV. A variety of different touch receptors embedded in the skin register pressure, pain, hot and cold, but it is only with time and experience that we learn to assign *meaning* to what we touch: our mother's soft cheek versus a hot frying pan. Cells in the retina of the eye respond selectively to edges and rounded fields. But the raw data they convey do not become vision without higher levels of integration in the brain, and these require learning. Tiny hair cells in the cochlea of the inner ear respond selectively to different frequencies of sound, but again, only with practice do we learn to organize these and "hear" them as a professor's lecture or a Mozart sonata. And if a particular sound distinction does not exist in a language, as with the English "R" and "L" sounds in Japanese, it will not be heard by adult users of that language. It will not exist for them. (Interestingly, the distinction can still be heard if the sounds are presented purely as sounds, and not in the context of speech. Once again, context determines meaning.)

Along similar lines, but in the opposite direction, we know that there are South American birds capable of seeing into the ultraviolet range of light, beyond the frequencies seen by the human eye. What might that look like? We have no idea; it simply does not exist in the world as we perceive it. Dogs have vastly more sensitive hearing than we do, and their sense of smell is so finely tuned that they can be trained to detect mere molecules of chemical explosives and cancer cells. They know when another dog has marked territory, and they leave their mark in return: an olfactory handshake of sorts, but one that persists over days. Dogs, then, perceive a different world. What is theirs like? Again, it's beyond our ability to know.

If we are to assign primacy to the mind, then it is essential to understand that the world brought to you by your five senses is in no way objective. Worse still, we cannot know for certain that *anything* exists "out there" independent of the mind, because all our information is subjective—filtered, transduced, or perhaps even manufactured by the senses and the brain. For all we know, we could be making the whole thing up! This is the doctrine known as *solipsism*: that the only thing we can truly be said to know is self. Solipsism is not popular; it is the bane of philosophers and scientists alike. But perhaps that's because it's impossible to disprove. The idea that what we perceive is "real" in any absolute sense is a fiction, a convenient construct that we all buy into. But we pay a price for that—an enormous price. We remain blinded to what we're missing. Worse still, we deny that there *is* anything missing.

A Course in Miracles tells us over and over that in fact we're missing the whole show. We are so captivated by the perceived world that we fail to recognize a far greater reality, one that exists internally, within the mind. Our dependency on perception has grievous costs and consequences. Because if the ego's world is real, then there is no room for the reality of spirit. Remember, you run either OS1 or OS2, and never both simultaneously. If the ego and its world of perception are what's real—your baseline reality, so to speak—then you are condemned to "*a senseless wandering, without a purpose and without accomplishment of any kind.*"[4] Your hopes of happiness will be dashed again and again. You will never achieve fulfillment, because you're searching under the wrong streetlight, outside yourself in a world of shifting perceptions untethered from the truth within.

> *The world's perception . . . rests on differences: on uneven background and shifting foreground, on unequal heights and diverse sizes, on varying degrees of darkness and light, and thousands of contrasts in which each thing seen competes with every other in order to be recognized. A larger object overshadows a smaller one. A brighter thing draws the attention from another with less intensity of appeal. And a more threatening idea, or one conceived of as more desirable by the world's standards, completely upsets the mental balance. What the body's eyes behold is only conflict. Look not to them for peace and understanding.*[5]

The Past as Context

The workings of Never-Mind may begin with the body's five senses, but they do not end there. In order to make meaning of the world we perceive, we utilize more complex, higher-order mechanisms to process the raw data brought to us by our senses. We make judgments and comparisons. These are necessarily based on past experience. And they block us from knowing truth far more effectively than anything the senses can offer up.

Our brains are designed for learning. Once we interpret a particular experience in a certain way, we are far more inclined to interpret other experiences in the same way. We have learned from the experience. If we climb a steep hill with great difficulty and then spy another in the distance, we anticipate, quite reasonably, that the climb will be just as hard. As a result, we may try to avoid that hill by searching for a way around it. If we're awakened from sleep by an unfamiliar noise, one we can't easily categorize, we may suspect burglars. We may grab a flashlight to go check, or a gun if we own one. We may lock ourselves in the bathroom, terrified. Or we might dismiss it as nothing, roll over, and go back to sleep. How we respond will depend on what we've learned from past experience—our context for making sense of the sound. Someone who's lived for decades in an old house full of unusual creaks is more likely to overlook it than someone who's just moved in. But past experience becomes interwoven with our identity, that is, our life story. An ex-Marine who's seen combat will react differently than an infirm eighty-year-old widow or a teen who was raped at night in her bedroom. Their differing past experiences tell them who they are and determine their range of options for responding.

One afternoon my wife and I were sitting on our back deck, which looked out over a small wooded area. One tree had partially fallen on another and was leaning precariously, held up only by the strong limbs of its neighbor. I mused out loud that we should probably cut it down. The healthier tree must be under a terrible strain from supporting so much weight. What relief it would feel to be freed from its burden. My wife cried out, "No! We can't cut it down. The other tree will feel so lonely." Our different psychological makeups, rooted in our childhoods, led us to view the two trees in very opposite ways: burden versus companionship, relief versus loneliness. If such differences arise between two people in a loving marriage, is it any wonder the world is so rife with conflict? (And in case you're wondering, we left the two trees standing unharmed. Or we left them to fend for themselves. It depends on your point of view.)

Our reliance on the past to give meaning to what we see in the present applies even to the simplest of items. This allows *A Course in Miracles* to make the bold assertion that we do not see anything as it truly is—we see only the past—and to back it up with the following line of reasoning.

Look at a cup, for example. Do you see a cup, or are you merely reviewing your past experience of picking up a cup, being thirsty, drinking from a cup, feeling the rim of a cup against your lips, having breakfast, and so on? Are not your aesthetic reactions to the cup, too, based on past experiences? How else would you know whether or not this kind of cup will break if you drop it? What do you know about this cup except what you learned in the past? You would have no idea what this cup is, except for your past learning. Do you, then, really see it?[6]

It is impossible to view any object—even a simple cup—much less to interpret complex events, without recruiting the past to give meaning.

Past experience becomes particularly powerful when it frightens us, injures us, or harms someone close to us. If you were mugged at gunpoint on a dark street in a bad part of town, you might become anxious if a friend suggests checking out a nightclub in that same area. That neighborhood has become a trigger for fear. *Something bad happened here once, and therefore it could happen again.* Such learning is advantageous to survival. We've formed an association that triggers anxiety, but that anxiety is useful because it warns us away from a potentially dangerous situation. But notice: each time you form such an association, your view of the world constricts. It hardens into a mold predetermined by past experience. You import the fear you felt back then into the present. You keep it alive by anticipating its recurrence. The world you perceive increasingly becomes defined by threat, danger, and suffering. You are less likely to explore new parts of the city, especially if they have a bad reputation. You're ruled by fear, not fun.

In the 1980s I evaluated a young Vietnamese man who complained of terrible headaches in the wake of a motorbike accident. But his scans and studies were entirely normal. None of his specialist physicians could determine the cause of his headaches, so they referred him to me, a psychiatrist.

With the help of a translator, I conducted a long and careful interview. The first thing I discovered was that this man did not in fact have headaches, not as we think of them. He had *head pain* that lingered from his accident. The second was that, as a young child, he had lived through the Vietnam war. An uncle of his had been hit in the head by shrapnel. He'd seemed to recover without incident, but continued to complain of head pain. Months after his injury, the uncle died suddenly with no explanation. When my patient experienced continuing head pain following his accident, he assumed that the same fate awaited him, but was too frightened to tell anyone. Each morning he peered into the mirror, wondering if this day was to be his last, afraid he'd suddenly collapse and die on the spot like his uncle. For this man, because of his past experience, head pain that persisted after an injury was equivalent to a death sentence. As a result, the pain was more urgent. It caused him more suffering.

Once I'd brought the association with his uncle to light, he and I could discuss it. I explained the significant differences between his condition and his deceased uncle's. With this new information in hand, whenever he felt the head pain he could enlarge his context beyond his uncle's death and so overcome his fear. As a result, the worry about his pain decreased dramatically. He no longer interpreted it as a harbinger of death. It still hurt, but it carried no threat. Consequently, the pain itself lessened. In a short time, it disappeared completely.

When you believe something, you have made it true for you.[7]

Networks and Knowing

While driving through the American Southwest, visitors are struck by the profusion of arroyos: deeply gouged crevices that crisscross the barren landscape. These can range in size from simple gullies to canyons over fifty feet deep and one hundred fifty feet wide. The ground in the desert is, of course, very dry. When it rains hard, water washes over the ground and carries off considerable amounts of soil with it, eventually carving out a channel. Each new storm refills these channels and carves them ever more deeply into the arid landscape. Once present, an arroyo will not disappear; it will only grow wider and deeper.

A similar process takes place in the brain. Some event occurs. Its sensory components ("What was that strange sound?") and your cognitive interpretation (that is, the meaning you assign to it: "It must be a burglar") are encoded in the brain by activating a particular pathway of neurons: a neural network. When another, similar incident occurs, it is more likely to activate and follow that same neuronal pathway, just like water flowing into and deepening the arroyo. This holds true for simple perceptions—for example, four legs plus a tail and barking equals *dog*, whether that's a Chihuahua or Great Dane—as well as more complex patterns of behavior. It's a characteristic of brain function: all experience is self-reinforcing.

I once treated a woman who, the moment she walked through my office door for her first session, informed me that there was no way she could work with me. "Why is that?" I asked. "Because you're tall. And you have black hair. I was abused by a man who was tall with dark hair." This woman had learned in a rather primitive way to associate these two aspects of one particular male's appearance with painful abuse. Her eyes registered *tall* and *black hair*, and her neural networks did the rest, directly linking these traits to *abuser*. She was caught in a self-reinforcing loop. I countered by pointing out that I also wore glasses and had a goatee. Was that true of her abuser? "No," she said, as if it were a striking revelation. "I guess I can work with you after all."

By introducing new information, I cracked her out of the neuronal loop established by her traumatic past. But notice: had I *not* given her new information, had I allowed her to flee my office in a panic, not only would nothing have changed in her loop, it would have grown stronger. Her faith in its predictive power and its ability to save her from harm would have increased, because in her mind she would once again have encountered a tall, dark-haired abuser and managed to escape. As with the arroyos of the Southwest, every storm etches them more deeply into the ground.

Perception seems to teach you what you see. Yet it but witnesses to what you taught. It is the outward picture of a wish: an image that you wanted to be true.[8]

There's a common saying that, to a hammer, everything looks like a nail. A layperson shrugs off aches that to a doctor's ears warn of disease, accurately or not. A lawyer writes up a contract anticipating all that could possibly go wrong, then extends that vigilance to her boyfriend's behavior, even though conflict in relationships is unavoidable and not governable by contract. A master chef cannot eat a meal without evaluating which ingredients and spices have contributed to its taste and how it might be improved upon. Each has come to view their world in a certain way, selectively focusing on what they have learned to judge as important. But none of them started out like that.

None of us are born "hammers." We have to learn. Our neural networks adapt, then adapt some more, until finally they are certain that they know what they're processing and lock it in. Now, instead of adapting to new information, they work to assimilate it and make it fit into their preconceived framework. The doctor can't stop herself from applying what she knows to her children, making them unnecessarily fearful of disease. The attorney terminates good, caring relationships over trivial breaches of her unspoken contract. ("He was ten minutes late—again!—and we almost missed the movie. That's inconsiderate. I'm done with him.") When neural networks grow too rigid and become unable to incorporate anything new, anything outside the scope of prior learning, we become prisoners of our pasts.

At this point everything truly does start to look like a nail. We can see only what our pasts have taught us to see. What we *don't* see is deemed untrue, or worse, nonexistent. We resist it. Anyone who disagrees with us is a fool whose opinion can be dismissed. Or worse, they're a threat and should be eliminated.

*   *   *

We can better understand neural networks if we borrow a concept from the world of computers. When you link together several different functions on your computer and activate them all with a single keystroke, it's called a *macro*. Now, instead of having to perform five different, separate operations, you assign them all to one key, tap it, and voilà, all five operations are performed automatically in sequence, saving you time and effort.

Perception works in much the same way. After we've seen a number of dogs, we no longer have to run through a perceptual algorithm that concludes: *four legs* + *tail* + *barking* = *dog*. We simply "see" a dog. Same for cars. Faces. Houses. Rooms. You get the picture.

A neural network is a macro of sorts that shunts a particular set of perceptions down a preexisting pathway that automatically assigns them meaning based on prior experience—with no conscious thought required. Think of it as a convenience. We are spared the effort of having to actually think and process what we perceive, but at the cost of a broader awareness. This holds true not only for our personal lives, but for the world in which we live as well.

Perception Sliced and Diced

If you drive to work, when you climb into your car in the morning, do you have to think about how you'll get there?

Of course not. You follow the route you know. You might make minor adjustments for road conditions like traffic, snow, or an accident, and you would certainly notice if a Ferrari or an ambulance happened to scream past you. But during that drive, the road becomes your entire world, and it unspools before you in predictable segments: first your neighborhood, then the freeway, the exit ramp, more streets, and finally the parking lot for your workplace. What goes unnoticed is the contour of the land on which the road was built. You drive over culverts with flowing streams beneath and never know it. You climb hills and navigate curves with little awareness. In a city, with its grid of streets and tall buildings, you may not even know the position of the sun or the direction in which you're headed.

From a different perspective, like flying over the landscape in a plane, you see not individual roads and their surroundings, but the land in its entirety: the towns, their industrial areas, streams and woodlands, hills and valleys, all viewed simultaneously within the same frame. From above, the larger context is restored. It's one reason why flying is so exhilarating.

We disrupt the natural contour of the land not only with roads, but also by dividing it up into parcels of property on which we construct houses and buildings, each assigned its own street number. These houses and buildings reside within distinct communities, towns and cities, which in turn are part of counties, states, and countries. Each has its own history, its own dialect and accent, its particular style of cooking, and its own customs and laws. And yet the borders that define and separate them, like all things of ego, are wholly artificial.

The artificial nature of borders is beautifully illustrated in a scene from French director Jean Renoir's classic 1937 film *La Grande Illusion*. Two French prisoners of war, one from a wealthy family, the other working-class, become good friends despite their differences. Together they escape from a World War I prison camp. Their goal is to make it safely out of Germany into neutral Switzerland. In the film's final scene, they make a run for the Swiss border, crossing a wide snow-covered field. There is a panoramic shot of two tiny dark figures struggling forward amid a vast expanse of white snow. A German soldier spies them and raises his rifle to shoot. Another soldier stops him, telling him that they've crossed the border into Switzerland. The border is invisible: nothing to see but the unblemished field of snow. And yet a matter of mere yards determines life and death. This is not just a fluke of wartime. Accidentally stray across the border from Colorado into Nebraska while smoking marijuana and you could wind up in jail for a long time.

It is in the nature of the ego to separate and draw distinctions where none exist, because the ego is itself the child of separation: its own willful departure from the oneness that is God. The ego carves out its world of perception apart from and in opposition to oneness, and then further divides and subdivides it into myriads of different people, things, and events. Each time we look out and see this world of separate things, we cannot help but make comparisons between them, thereby strengthening the ego's iron grip over us. Yet the differences and distinctions are mere artifice. Their dizzying variety blinds us to their true purpose, namely, to keep us unconscious, oblivious to the reality of God and spirit. We fear that without the world we know, all would be chaos. Yet the Course assures us that *"without the ego, all would be love."*[9]

The ego takes the same slice-and-dice approach to the concept of time. The actual passage of time is really quite fluid and highly subjective. If your doctor is running behind and you're stuck waiting in her office for hours with nothing to entertain you but ancient copies of *People* magazine, time trickles by. But when you're engaged in some fun activity like a sport or a good movie, it seems to fly. However, we don't conceptualize time this way. We carve the day up into hours, minutes, and seconds. And we bundle our days into weeks, months, and years. This imposes a certain uniformity, but it's completely artificial.

I've participated in weeklong workshops where they collected watches and phones at the door and didn't return them until the workshop ended. The sense of time passing was very different, and quite freeing. When we tie our routines to the hour of the day, we're forced to comply with an inflexible schedule that tells us when we should be working, eating, and sleeping; when we need to get moving; and when we can chill and relax. It overrides our natural rhythms in much the same way that the street grid does the landscape.

Cross from one time zone into another and what has changed? You've driven a mile and yet suddenly you gain or lose an hour in your day. The state of Arizona does not observe Daylight Savings Time. Yet the Navaho Nation, residing within the borders of Arizona, does; while the Hopi tribe, whose borders are contained within Navaho Nation territory, does not. Drive across Arizona in the summer and the time bounces back and forth by an hour so often that it becomes meaningless. There's no point in trying to keep up.

I once flew from Auckland, New Zealand to Honolulu on New Year's Eve. Because my flight crossed the International Date Line, I celebrated New Year's Eve with a bottle of Scotch at the airport in Auckland and then arrived in Hawaii on the morning of New Year's Eve, which I proceeded to celebrate for a second time later that night. The conventions governing time turn out to be even more arbitrary than the boundaries separating states and countries.

Of course, these artificial constructs have their benefits as well. Before there were roads, people had to make their way on foot or horseback over rough terrain. The views may have been prettier, but it was also very easy to get lost. And without our system of timekeeping, we could not function as a society. It would be difficult to meet up with friends for dinner or book an airline flight, much less have everyone show up for work "on time" at the same hour.

The mental structures imposed on us by the Never-Mind help us to function in its world of time and space. But they also restrict us, herding us down familiar byways into a consensus "reality" that diverts us from whatever truth might actually lie beyond, whether that's the actual lay of the land, the natural ebb and flow of time, or the spacious, unbounded Ever-Mind.

Deconstructing Macros

If you've ever tried to learn to play a sport like baseball, golf, or tennis, you know how easy it is to fall into bad habits. Without intending it, your swing takes on a characteristic hitch specific to your build, musculature, and native ability. As you get used to that swing, however, you'll tend to rely on it more and more, despite the hitch. (This is another example of neural networks in action.) It's gotten you this far and made you a competent player. All well and good. You've developed a macro with an unnecessary hitch in the middle. Big deal. When a fastball comes streaking toward the plate at high velocity, there isn't time to contemplate the mechanics of your swing. You *want* the macro, the neural net, to take control.

However, if that hitch in your swing is limiting you and keeping you from becoming a better player, you'll need to correct it. In order to achieve this, you'll have to examine closely what it is you're doing wrong. You'll need to deconstruct the old macro before you can replace it with a new one. You'll need to reprogram the neural network. This turns out to be harder than we realize, and almost impossible to manage on our own, because we lack the perspective. We can't play and observe ourselves at the same time. It's why we have trainers and coaches. Their task is to spot what we're doing wrong, point it out to us, and suggest better alternatives.

In my mid-thirties, I started taking guitar lessons from a highly skilled performer. In order to demonstrate a particular series of finger picks to me, he had to slow them way down. He had to deconstruct his own patterned learning—to disassemble his macros. I watched his frustration mount as he struggled to become consciously aware again of what his fingers had been doing automatically for decades.

Think about it this way: How long would you say it took you to learn how to walk? You don't remember, but I promise you it was not an instant success. You stood up on wobbly legs, you cruised along gripping the edges of coffee tables and couches, you clutched at your parents' hands while taking tentative, halting steps. And you fell. Often. All in order to learn to coordinate your leg muscles in exactly the right way to maintain balance and propel yourself forward. Eventually you got it down pat. You could run, skip, and jump without giving it so much as a thought. Now stand up. Take a few short steps and tell me *exactly* what your leg muscles are doing. You can't. It's not possible. The macro is too well established, too ingrained to be deconstructed. But if you suffered a stroke and had to learn to walk all over again, you'd be paying exquisite attention to those muscles and what they were doing.

Along the same lines, try to monitor the motion of your tongue when you speak. You are controlling it, obviously, but it doesn't feel that way. You merely think the words, and your tongue produces them automatically through a complex series of movements learned when you were around two or three years old and now linked together as macros. And once again, if a stroke knocked out the part of your brain that controlled speech, or if you moved to a foreign country where they speak a different language, you'd have to relearn those tongue movements all over again in order to build new macros in a slow and painstaking process.

If you want to learn a new language, play a new instrument, or improve your tennis game by changing your grip, you won't find it easy. Those old neural nets resist change. Remember, that's what they're designed to do. It's as if the thousands of repetitions from the past have created their own gravitational field, and it pulls you back into the old pattern whether you like it or not. The fact is, we instinctively hold on to what feels familiar and comfortable, because *it's always worked before*. We don't want to test out a new batting stance with bases loaded in the bottom of the ninth—and risk striking out. We're embarrassed when tennis balls soar over the fence or we plow that drive into the rough on consecutive holes, because we're trying out a new grip. We prefer to revert to our old standby grip. It may limit us, but it won't embarrass us. We only make a change if we're truly committed to becoming a better player.

This holds true not only for sports and music. It applies equally to how we conduct ourselves in relationships. We develop certain expectations, certain patterns of behavior, based on early life experience (usually what we witnessed from our parents). We then unconsciously carry these bad habits into adulthood. We suppress anger like dad did—until it explodes in a storm of rage. We manipulate like mom and her sisters. We lavish attention on our partner, hoping that they'll appreciate our efforts and do the same for us in return. We drown our inhibitions and anxieties in alcohol. We dig those arroyos deeper and deeper. Such learned habits block us from engaging in honest, fully loving relationships. We resist making changes, of course, because we don't want to admit that there's anything wrong with us or the way we're behaving. Sometimes we'd prefer not to even look at the problem; we flare into anger if it's pointed out to us.

Unlike sports, where at least we can admit we've developed a hitch in our swing and get help, relationships come with a convenient, prepackaged scapegoat: our partner. It's far easier to pin the blame on them for whatever's gone wrong than to take a hard look at our own flawed beliefs and behaviors. As a result, we're also more reluctant to seek help. Consulting a couples therapist carries more of a stigma than signing up for lessons with the golf pro. We stick to our entrenched position, needing to be "right," rather than trying to change and find happiness. And so we do not change. We judge and blame and attack. We divert and ignore and put up a false front. We keep whacking at the relationship with that same faulty swing again and again, and we're surprised and infuriated when we get the same result and our partner fails to change. We may even find a new partner, someone who loves and accepts us just the way we are, bad habits and all. And the cycle begins again.

The Never-Mind thrives on this sort of automaticity. For if we ever did slow down and deconstruct our macros, if we looked deeply into the beliefs that make up our worldview, we would expose their weakness. And once exposed, we would no longer be captive to them. We might try a new approach, a more effective swing, a better way. It is precisely this that *A Course in Miracles* attempts to teach us, but applied to perception in its entirety. And it is this that the ego will battle to its dying breath.

Finding the Present

The value of macros and neural networks lies in their ability to codify experience without our consciously having to think about it. We recognize the dog as a dog and stoop to pet it; we are wary of tall men with dark hair and keep our distance accordingly. But this is also the danger of macros. They offer a perceptual shortcut. They lead us directly to a conclusion, an interpretation of *what is* that's anchored solidly in the past, without requiring us to test that belief in the present. They make an end-run around awareness and in so doing, they limit our capacity to choose a different response.

In essence, we have bartered the present for the past: overriding present experience with beliefs learned long ago. This keeps us bound to the past. We remain its prisoner in the truest sense. Whether out of fear or habit, we allow the Never-Mind to continue to have its way with us, like a mad dictator who holds onto power by scaring his people with tales of terrorism. *I alone can keep you safe. Without me, terrible things will happen. You will starve. You will perish. I alone can protect you. Trust me!* We believe him and give up our power. Or we don't fully believe, but feel it's too much trouble to risk challenging him.

To counter the Never-Mind and loosen its death grip on the past, Buddhists advocate a practice known as *beginner's mind*. This involves intentionally suspending everything you've learned from the past in order to perceive the world anew, as if you were encountering it for the very first time. When you drive a particular route for the first time, you are active and engaged. You notice its scenic beauty and the interesting shops along the roadside. You make a mental note of intersections and landmarks, tricky curves, the location of service stations.

Likewise, when you meet someone you're attracted to for the first time, you tune in to the way they look at you. You really listen to what they say: not just their words, but the nuances, the voice tones. You care; you're interested, engaged. Once you've gotten to know them, however, your impressions become restricted to the familiar image of them that you've built up in your mind from past experience. The macro has taken over. The past has superseded the present.

Beginner's mind returns you to the present moment, where everything is fresh and new and where the door to Ever-Mind stands perpetually open. Your neural networks were shaped by the past, but *you* do not live there. Only the present moment exists. If we want happiness, it can only meet us where we live, in the *now*, not in some memory of the past or a fantasy of the future based on the past.

Shifting Perception

We've seen how perception is not possible without context and contrast; how it depends on past experience, encoded in neural networks and macros, to give meaning to what is perceived; how it overwrites the present with the past; and how resistant it is to change. But let's face it: the world of perception is what we know. It's all we've ever known. We may be its prisoners, but is there really an alternative?

It *is* possible to escape from the self-reinforcing neural networks that govern perception, but only if we are open to receiving new information. This comes to us through new experience that is markedly different from the past. My Vietnamese patient had to meet with an American psychiatrist to learn that he would not share his uncle's fate. My grandfather had to cross an ocean to discover the sports reel that exposed the Bolsheviks' lie.

By enlarging our context to include new information, we change the nature of what we perceive. My grandfather would never again mistake a football for a loaf of bread. The same can be said for the Vietnamese man and his head pain, or for the female patient who mistook me for an abuser. Once their understanding shifted as a result of new information, they could never again interpret head pain as fatal or tall, dark-haired therapists as predators, at least not without further evidence.

But the change runs deeper than that, because when perception changes as a result of new information, *the perceiver is changed as well*. Both patients emerged from treatment with an experience of overcoming fear. This creates its own, new neural network. Going forward, the likelihood of that old fear being retriggered was significantly reduced. But more significantly, each now had a basis in experience for believing that they could overcome other fears as well. They became less prone to fear, less willing to fall into the victim role. They experienced themselves as stronger people. When our worldview changes, our self-concept changes too.

> *The world is nothing in itself. Your mind must give it meaning. . . . There is no world apart from what you wish, and herein lies your ultimate release. Change but your mind on what you want to see, and all the world must change accordingly.*[10]

However, *A Course in Miracles* calls into question whether *any* experience can be considered truly new and different if it reinforces your identification with the ego. No matter how much you try to enlarge context, as long as you remain tied to the world of perception and Never-Mind, they will continue to dominate and control you. No matter how strong you build your house or how much money you sock away, you will never feel completely safe and at peace in a world designed to be fearful by its maker, the ego. Hire the best physicians and personal trainers, take the perfect combination of nutritional supplements, and still, your health will not be guaranteed. Worse, whatever you do, wherever you travel or choose to live, whoever you befriend, your body will still die eventually. That's guaranteed. The ego lets you "choose your poison"—but is choice among poisons really any choice at all? We've been so conditioned into believing that the world we perceive is real, and that this is a given about which we have no choice, that we don't bother to look for an alternative.

The surest way to keep someone imprisoned is to convince them that there is no prison and they're free to do whatever they choose. Why would anyone attempt to escape from what they think does not exist? The popular 1999 film *The Matrix* depicts a world identical to ours, but which turns out to be a giant computer simulation: a virtual-reality prison. Only a very few realize this. Because the simulation is so accurate, so real, it is practically impossible to escape from on your own. You must get help from outside, from someone who already knows that the Matrix is a lie because they've broken free of its confounding illusions, someone who will share their knowledge with you in order to help you escape as well.

In the film, that help comes in the form of human beings who live outside the computer simulation. In *A Course in Miracles*, it comes from the Holy Spirit. The Holy Spirit lives outside the world of perception. It does not participate in the games played by the ego or Never-Mind, but it does recognize them for the usurpers they are, and it reaches out to us despite their resistance in order to help us free ourselves.

The Course describes the Holy Spirit as the bridge between the ego's world of perception and what it calls the *real world*, a world cleansed of the influence of ego and primed to return us to our true Self as God's Son. This Self exists outside the limits of time, never having left the eternal oneness of God. We will have more to say about the real world in the next chapter.

The Holy Spirit is an aspect of the Ever-Mind. It is there to help us awaken—but only if we ask for help. We have free will. As the Course states in its introduction:

Free will does not mean that you can establish the curriculum. It means only that you can elect what you want to take at a given time.[11]

We can choose to believe in what does not exist, even if it hurts us. We can run the ego's race, chasing its ever-receding finish line, for as long as we like. The Holy Spirit waits patiently, in the knowledge that eventually our suffering will bring us to our knees and we will reach out for help. But we can expedite this process.

The Pitfalls of Judgment

Given that we have become the willing prisoners of Never-Mind, then exactly what is it that keeps us imprisoned? If we can identify those factors, we will have a much better chance of breaking free.

In the ego's world of perception where context and contrast dominate, it is almost impossible not to make judgments. These can be as simple as comparing sizes or as complex as choosing a new home. Most often, our judgments are about other people: people we know or public figures we've heard or read about. We also make judgments about global situations and about challenges we face in our own personal lives.

Such judgments provide the fodder for the inner monologue: that voice inside our head that masquerades as *self*. It's a nonstop torrent of judgment: how we feel about life, why we're justified in feeling that way, what others think of us, what we want from them, what they want from us, how we should behave in order to get what we want, and of course, how to keep safe and stay out of danger.

> *Perception is a continual process of accepting and rejecting, organizing and reorganizing, shifting and changing. Evaluation is an essential part of perception, because judgments are necessary in order to select.*
>
> *What happens to perceptions if there are no judgments and nothing but perfect equality? Perception becomes impossible. Truth can only be known. All of it is equally true, and knowing any part of it is to know all of it.*[12]

If we want to experience peace, if we want to escape from the ego and silence the voice of Never-Mind, then we must free ourselves from judgment. Without judgment, we can no longer be so certain about what's right or best—for us, or for anyone else. We recognize that we are limited in our inability to understand what anything really means. We may not be able to stop ourselves from judging, but we can at least begin to question the validity of our judgments and take them less seriously. We no longer have to identify with them or incorporate them into our self-concept. As a result, the ego's hold on us is loosened enough to allow the Holy Spirit to enter and reinterpret things for us, in much the way that a wise parent might counsel a child about some upsetting schoolyard altercation.

Think about it this way: The human mind is incapable of understanding the full context of any circumstance. The central purpose of this chapter is to demonstrate that whatever we see, or think we see, will necessarily be contaminated by our past experience. Therefore, we are un-doubtedly missing things. Important things.

A Course in Miracles makes a powerful case for the fu-tility of all judgments.

> *The aim of our curriculum, unlike the goal of the world's learning, is the recognition that judgment in the usual sense is impossible. This is not an opinion, but a fact. In order to judge anything rightly, one would have to be fully aware of an inconceivably wide range of things: past, present and to come. One would have to recognize in advance all the effects of his judgments on everyone and everything involved in them in any way. And one would have to be certain there is no distortion in his perception, so that his judgment would be wholly fair to everyone on whom it rests now and in the future. Who is in a position to do this? Who except in gran-diose fantasies would claim this for himself?*
>
> *Remember how many times you thought you knew all the "facts" you needed for judgment, and how wrong you were! Is there anyone who has not had this experience? Would you know how many times you merely thought you were right, without ever realizing you were wrong? Why would you choose such an arbitrary basis for decision making? Wisdom is not judgment; it is the relinquishment of judgment.*[13]

And, in a more succinct summation:

> *To judge is to be dishonest, for to judge is to assume a po-sition you do not have. Judgment without self-deception is impossible.*[14]

*   *   *

In any circumstance where you choose to exercise your own judgment, you engage in self-deception. You buy into the delusion that you have sufficient information to render judgment when in fact you do not. In effect, you pretend that you are God.

A respected professor at a well-known university related the following story at a *Course in Miracles* study group. He was teaching a popular class to hundreds of undergraduates. While lecturing, he quite reasonably expected that his students would remain silent. If they had questions, they would save them for the end of class. One day a young woman entered and seated herself in the front row of the large lecture hall. There seemed to be something not quite right about her. Indeed, in the middle of his lecture she thrust her hand into the air and waved it about. She had a question. He ignored her, but she would not be deterred, and finally he halted his lecture and called on her. She asked her question, he answered, and then resumed his lecture. A short time later she raised her hand again to ask another question. He reminded her to please wait and talk to him after class. But when the lecture concluded, she did not wait; she left the room in a hurry. At the next class the following week, there she was again seated in the front row, and again she interrupted his lecture and peppered him with questions. He couldn't believe her rudeness. Striving to hold his temper and remain polite, he answered her. This pattern continued for several more classes. The professor grew less troubled by her presence. He knew her routine and was in fact getting somewhat used to it. Then all of a sudden, she was absent. She didn't show up the next week either, or the week after that. He made inquiries. And what he learned was that this young woman had desperately wanted to audit his class. Why? Because she was dying and knew she'd never have another chance. The reason for her abrupt absence was that she had succumbed to her illness and passed away. His judgments about her and her rude, intrusive behavior had been accurate as far as his information went. But he'd missed the larger context of her illness. He lacked essential information when he made his judgment about her. Had he known, he would have felt and behaved very differently.

This professor gives us a dramatic example of the problem with judgment, even those judgments that seem perfectly justified, self-evident even. You probably have not experienced anything like this professor's story. However, you have made judgments that were untrue and which you later regretted, of that I am certain. Perhaps you've sat in a restaurant waiting far too long for your order to arrive and wondered what on earth was the problem with your waiter. When the food finally arrived cold, your anger boiled over. You left a lousy tip to make your point. Yet you never considered whether this was his first night on the job, or whether he'd just learned before his shift began that his mother had been in an accident, or whether he's sick but trying to work in spite of it, because he can't afford not to. Perhaps you cursed the woman who blew by you on the freeway, then abruptly cut across three lanes of traffic to exit. Was she a terrible driver? An aggressive, entitled one-percenter? Or was she rushing to her child's school or the hospital for an emergency? And what of the doctor who always seems to run an hour late for appointments, leaving you to stew irritated and bored in her waiting room? Is she unprofessional and slow? A poor planner? Or might she care so much about her patients' well-being that she's willing to fall behind in her schedule in order to render the best care she's capable of?

As a psychotherapist, I've had the experience more than once of treating someone who makes frequent and serious complaints about their spouse. My mind forms a mental picture of the spouse. They are controlling, abusive, distant and judgmental, hopelessly preoccupied with work, or clueless about the most basic requirements of being in relationship. At some point, we agree to bring the spouse into the therapy session and I discover—much to my surprise and delight—that they're nothing like what I'd pictured. My judgments were based on limited, subjective, and necessarily biased information.

This penchant for judgment goes beyond merely missing the fuller context of a situation. It reflects a willingness—an enjoyment even—in being right, in standing pat in the certainty that you know how people are and how the world works, and nothing will change that. The first step in moving past judgment then lies in the simple recognition that you do not have all the facts. You are far from omniscient. Therefore, your judgments will *always* be faulty. *They will not work,* and this turns out to be the best reason for letting them go. (We are not talking here about routine decisions like when it's safe to cross the street or whether you should wear a raincoat. The judgments that get us in trouble involve other people and the assumptions we make about them.) Judgment is flawed if it comes from the ego and not from the Holy Spirit. Attempt to rely on your own judgment, according to *A Course in Miracles*, and you throw away any chance at lasting peace.

The Ultimate Context

We need to take the process of relinquishing judgment still deeper, however. This will require an important admission on your part, namely, that you are incapable of making accurate judgments *because you are thoroughly identified with the ego*. You are not in your right mind; you suffer from self-deception, quite literally. But Ever-Mind and the Holy Spirit are also part of you. They have not abandoned you. They look out upon the same world you see, observing it from a higher vantage, and with only one goal: to set you free and bring you peace.

Ever-Mind becomes the final, ultimate context against which all else, the entire world of perception, is to be weighed. It doesn't reinterpret just one small fragment of perception by slightly enlarging the context. It applies to *everything,* your entire world. It reinterprets all of it in the clear light of unchanging and unchangeable truth. This is the Course's plan of the Atonement. It reverses the mind's split from oneness and God. This is salvation.

> *A dream of judgment came into the mind that God created perfect as Himself. And in that dream was Heaven changed to hell, and God made enemy unto His Son. How can God's*

Son awaken from the dream? It is a dream of judgment. So must he judge not, and he will awaken.[15]

How does this work? How do you free yourself from judgment? It seems impossible, but the Course maintains that the world we see and judge is what's impossible. Finding release from that world is therefore not only possible, but necessary.

Take any aspect of the world of perception, any judgment you might make or hold about another person, any sort of conflict whatsoever. Now enlarge the context in order to "see" your situation through the eyes of the Holy Spirit. All He knows is truth and its attributes: peace, love, unity. Viewed against this ultimate backdrop, *all* things in this world of perception—*all* of the ego's fears and desires—are exposed as mere illusion. Nothingness. They can have no impact on the truth of Who You Are. Remember, God created His one Son in His likeness. And according to *A Course in Miracles*, you are that Son (along with everyone else). *"God is but love, and therefore so am I."*[16] If what you behold is not love, it is not worthy of you. It is not real. It does not exist. Period. This recognition releases you from the ego, its world, and all its effects.

Because of this ultimate perspective, the Holy Spirit is fully capable of making accurate decisions on your behalf. Your decisions, based on your judgments, will run aground and leave you stranded in the ego's nightmare. His will awaken you and set you free. His sole purpose, in fact, is to guide you so that you won't have to rely upon your own flimsy interpretations about things you can never truly understand. *A Course in Miracles* describes the function of the Holy Spirit as follows:

> *The Holy Spirit abides in the part of your mind that is part of the Christ Mind [or Ever-Mind]. He represents your Self and your Creator, Who are One. . . . He seems to be a Voice, for in that form He speaks God's Word to you. He seems to be a Guide through a far country, for you need that form of help. He seems to be whatever meets the needs you think you have. But He is not deceived when you perceive your self entrapped in needs you do not have. It is from these He would deliver you. It is from these that He would make you safe.*[17]

The Holy Spirit brings to you whatever experiences you need to help awaken. But He will not accede to needs you only think you have, needs which actually arise from ego. This is a key distinction. If you pray for what would in fact hinder you and hurt you, you will not receive it of the Holy Spirit. This is in your best interests, even though you may not see it that way at the time. If a ten year-old wants a pack of cigarettes or an assault rifle, no caring parent will agree. Personally, I can recall many a situation and relationship I desired and was denied for which I now feel, years later, no regret, only profound gratitude.

You do not have to call this aspect of Ever-Mind by the name *Holy Spirit* if you find that uncomfortable. Think of it in whatever way you like—call it Higher Self, Guardian Angel, Innate Wisdom, the Goddess, the Universe, or any other term you prefer—as long as it allows you to get out of the way and *ask for help*. We will look at this process again in more detail, along with its relationship to miracles, in chapter 6.

You don't know the true purpose of anything—that is, how to use it to awaken to truth, and nothing else. Because of your identification with ego, you no longer see things clearly. But this higher part of you does. Therefore *"your function here is only to decide against deciding what you want, in recognition that you do not know."*[18] According to the Course, this is the only decision any of us can make that has any real meaning or impact. Anything else is a covert choice for the ego and its compelling display of illusions. But choice among illusions, as we have noted, is no choice at all.

When you try to make your own decisions, you are like a young child dashing wildly and blindly across a busy city street. You may make it safely across, and may do so many times, but sooner or later you'll get hit by a car. If you step back and ask for help, however, in the recognition that you do not know how to cross busy streets, then the all-knowing, all-loving Holy Spirit will take you by the hand and lead you gently and safely across.

> *There is Someone with you Whose judgment is perfect. He does know all the facts: past, present and to come. He does know all the effects of His judgment on everyone and everything involved in any way. And He is wholly fair to everyone, for there is no distortion in His perception.*
>
> *Therefore lay judgment down, not with regret but with a sigh of gratitude.*[19]

You have never given any problem to the Holy Spirit He has not solved for you, nor will you ever do so. You have never tried to solve anything yourself and been successful. Is it not time you brought these facts together and made sense of them? [20]

Say to the Holy Spirit only, "Decide for me," and it is done. For His decisions are reflections of what God knows about you, and in this light, error of any kind becomes impossible. [21]

No matter how much we enlarge our context, so long as it continues to rely on perception *in any form*, we will not understand what we are doing. We will wander lost, ignorant of truth. We will not experience peace. And whatever happiness we stumble upon will be fleeting and, in the end, unsatisfying. On the other hand, when we turn to the Holy Spirit and use His judgment as the final, ultimate context for navigating the world in which we live and move about, then peace, truth, freedom, and genuine, abiding happiness all become ours.

Through the Looking Glass

In Shakespeare's *As You Like It*, the character Jaques declares, "All the world's a stage, / And all the men and women merely players: / They have their exits and their entrances; / And one man in his time plays many parts." [22] We saw in chapter 1 that the Never-Mind indeed has us playing many parts, many roles, in order to divert us from discovering our true Self. Within the world of perception, we are playwright and director, actor and stage manager, for a host of illusory dramas. But if we are merely playing parts, acting out various roles, then we're led back to the central question from chapter 1—*Who are you?*—or, to take it a step further, what is the true nature of the self that plays these parts? And what happens if you drop your role? What if you decide to walk off the stage altogether? What lies beyond the curtain of perception?

> *Perception is a mirror, not a fact. And what I look on is my state of mind, reflected outward.*[23]

I was fortunate many years ago to attend a marvelous play with my young son. The opening scene was set in a Victorian drawing room with a huge fireplace in the background. Above the fireplace hung a large mirror that reflected the faces of the audience in the balcony above. Or so it appeared. The angle seemed wrong somehow. But the play commenced, and I forgot about the mirror. And then, not long into the play, something surprising took place. One of the characters leapt up, hurled a chair at the mirror, and shattered it with a flash and a loud BANG! Thick smoke choked the stage. When it cleared, the entire set had vanished. No drawing room, fireplace, or mirror. Instead, what was exposed behind the stage was a row of bleachers, and seated on the bleachers were thirty or forty additional audience members—the same ones I'd seen "reflected" in the mirror before it shattered. It turned out there never had been any mirror. It was a hole cut into the wall above the fireplace, framed to look like a mirror. As such, the people

I'd seen there were not a reflection. They were real. They would watch the remainder of the play from this different perspective, behind the now-open stage. This perceptual sleight of hand was perfectly suited to the play: *Through the Looking Glass.*[24] It was a marvelous entry into Wonderland, for Alice and for all of us in the audience.

The shattered mirror that was not a mirror offers a rich metaphor for the Ever-Mind in its relationship to the world of the senses. Break through the perceptual mirror, penetrate the mask of illusion, and what do you find? What awaits you on the other side? Reality: nothing more, nothing less.

> *Behind every image I have made, the truth remains unchanged. Behind every veil I have drawn across the face of love, its light remains undimmed. . . . God is still everywhere and in everything forever. And we who are part of Him will yet look past all appearances and recognize the truth beyond them.*[25]

PRACTICE

As an adult human being, you have become so reliant on your five senses and the world they portray that to attempt to look beyond them seems almost incomprehensible. But if you want to experience truth, it is necessary. The impostor Never-Mind works in tandem with the world of perception to keep us from seeing truly.

The nineteenth-century French poet Arthur Rimbaud made it his mission to disrupt the senses, hoping to blast his way through in order to seize truth and heaven. Unfortunately, the chief weapon in his arsenal was absinthe (a potent brew of alcohol, anise, and the toxic herb wormwood), and so a poor choice for this purpose. The writer Aldous Huxley took mescaline, a psychedelic drug, to pass through the "doors of perception" and experience a heightened sense of reality. American Indians embark on vision quests, Sufi dervishes whirl, monks meditate and intone chants, shamans soar to other realms on the rhythmic beat of drums. There are many, many avenues for disrupting the world of the senses, precisely because it turns out to be so much more fragile than we think.

The first month's lessons in the Course's Workbook for Students teach you to regard the world you see as meaningless and unreal: nothing but a fiction fabricated from your past. The Course then extends this teaching to include not only the world you perceive, but any and all thoughts you have about that world and your role in it. Here are a few examples.

Lesson 1: Nothing I see in this room means anything.
Lesson 3: I do not understand anything I see.
Lesson 4: These thoughts do not mean anything.
Lesson 7: I see only the past.
Lesson 9: I see nothing as it is now.
Lesson 11: My meaningless thoughts are showing me a meaningless world.
Lesson 25: I do not know what anything is for.

With each lesson, you are asked to apply the central idea to a random sampling of objects within your visual field or of thoughts that occupy your mind. You are not asked whether you agree with the lessons; it doesn't matter whether or not they make sense to you. You are only asked to apply them and assess the results down the line. There is a good reason for this: You are so stuck in what you think you see and understand that you have lost any ability to evaluate its truthfulness for yourself. As a result, you don't really know what's good for you and what's not. Like a compass that's been exposed for too long to a strong magnetic field, you can no longer point the way to true north.

In the practices that follow, you'll be given an opportunity to move beyond the world of perception and discover how thin its veneer really is. Pierce that veneer, peel it back, and you get a glimpse of what lies beyond, a taste of the true Self—a dip into Ever-Mind. We will go about this in two ways.

First, we will attempt to shift the context you apply to events, that is, the familiar framework of beliefs within which you try to interpret the things that happen to you.

We will then target perception at a more basic level, that of the senses, and like Rimbaud and Huxley, try to dislodge their hold on you (only without the use of drugs). There are many ways to trick the senses, to distract or overwhelm them, and in the process slip past these guardians of the Never-Mind. What I offer here is a small but representative sampling.

But first, a gentle caution. You've grown accustomed to the world as you currently see it. Even when it proves scary or painful, it's still solid and familiar, and the ego always prefers the known over the unknown. When this world begins to break apart, the feeling can be uplifting, but for some it can also provoke anxiety. Therefore, in the practices that follow, if at any time you find yourself feeling anxious rather than curious or relaxed, simply stop. If you experience eyestrain, stop. There is no need to push through. Only the ego would ask this of you and find fault if you discontinued because of discomfort.

Remember, the goal of these practices is to draw back the curtain of perception in order to expose the Never-Mind and its props. By doing so, you also invite the peace of Ever-Mind to enter. You want that peace. Whether you realize it or not, you want it more than anything this world has to offer. It is with this intent that I encourage you to try out these practices.

Practice One: Shifting Context

You should have paper and pencil or pen on hand to take notes.

Think about something upsetting that's recently occurred. This should not be a personal slight, like a friend's insult or lovers' quarrel, but something more global that's affected you strongly, like a natural disaster, mass shooting, or terrorist attack that you watched on TV; or even your team losing the Super Bowl or World Cup; or a major election in which your preferred candidate lost. Choose the first thing that comes to mind.

In as objective a manner as possible, step back from the incident and ask yourself why this event triggered such strong feelings in you.

- Were you hurt by it in any way? How, exactly?
- What, if anything, did you lose as a result?
- In what way did it cause you suffering?
- Do you anticipate further harm coming from it?
- Will it hurt you financially?
- Does it represent or rekindle some painful memory from your own past?
- Could it wind up actually killing you or someone you love?
- Does it bruise your identity by affronting some role or value you cherish?

Any and all of the above are acceptable reasons for your upset.

Now pick someone you know well and like, but whose personality is very different from yours. If you tend to be a pessimist, they are optimistic. If you are careful and analytic, they are impulsive and intuitive. And so on.

How might this event look to *her or him*? Step into their shoes. Would they be as upset as you are?

• If so, why? If not, what about it would they interpret differently?

• How might someone from another country see this event? Would their reaction be similar or different? Why?

• What if they were from somewhere very remote, with no Internet access and limited TV coverage? How might this change the way they felt about what occurred? Try their perspective on for size.

• What about someone from a war-ravaged nation like the Congo, Syria, or South Sudan? Would their familiarity with the horrors of war cause them to see this differently from you? Try to view this event through their eyes, in the context of their past experience.

• Would it make any difference if they practiced a different religion? How would a Buddhist respond to this event? A Muslim? An atheist?

• What if their race were different? Would that affect their interpretation?

Now, having tried on all of these different points of view, notice whether *your* feeling about this event has changed in any way. Did this process lessen or increase your sorrow and your anger? There is no right or wrong here. It's simply about observing the effect of different interpretive contexts.

• Now view this event as you would have ten years ago. What if anything would be different? How about twenty years ago? More?

- What if your child had been born on the same day that this incident occurred? Would that make it better? Worse? Or no different?
- How might your mother have felt about this event when *you* were a child? Or your father? What reactions might you have witnessed from them if this event had occurred back then? Is your reaction today similar in any way? Or different? And if so, why?
- Now jump ahead: How might this look and feel to you ten years from now? Twenty years? What's changed, if anything? And why?
- Finally, imagine this incident taking place on the last day of your life. You're dying—struggling for breath in a hospice or your own bed, surrounded by those who love you. How would you respond then? What would be different and why?

Now check in again. Have your feelings about this incident changed in any significant way? If so, what's different?

Practice Two: Loosening the Bonds of Perception

There are a number of parts to this practice. You will not be able to complete them all in one sitting, nor should you attempt this. Better to do one at a time. Once you've completed them all, you may find that some are more appealing or relaxing than others. Feel free to practice these as often as you like.

As we said before, if you experience any anxiety—stop. Take a break. Go outside and inhale the air. Stretch your arms and legs. Drink some water. Then later, give it another try. Or move on to the next practice and see how that one feels. If your discomfort persists, then skip this practice entirely and move on to the next chapter.

But you are far more likely to experience a comfortable sense of peace from these practices. They carve out space for your sense of self to expand—as if you'd been confined in a tight box and are now free to stand and move about. Be sure to ask your Higher Self—your Ever-Mind or Holy Spirit—to take charge and serve as your guide in these practices. It will let you know whether to proceed, take a break, or stop altogether and skip to the next chapter. And again, remember: there is no right or wrong in this. You are simply learning. Exploring. Discovering.

PART 1: RECOGNIZING PAST AND FUTURE IN PERCEPTION

Start by making sure you're seated comfortably. This first part of the practice works best if performed indoors at home. It is better to be sitting than standing or lying down.

Please read through the entire section before you start, and when you're confident you understand the instructions, put the book aside and give your full attention to the practice.

In a relaxed and casual way, look around you. Scan the room and everything in it. Don't let your glance rest too long on any one thing. Simply take in the room and all its contents.

Next, let your gaze settle randomly on any single object in the room. As you look at this object, ask yourself what meaning it has for you.

- What is its function, and how did you learn about that?
- When did you obtain it, and under what circumstances?
- Was it a gift or a purchase?
- If a gift, who gave it to you and on what occasion?
- If a purchase, what prompted you to buy it? Who was with you at the time? Was it expensive or a bargain?
- Are you happy with this object? Does it please you or bring up judgments? (For example, "I absolutely love that lamp, painting, piece of furniture," etc., or "That chair is hideous; it's embarrassing and threadbare; we need a new one; but can we afford it? Do I have the time to look for one?")

The thing to notice here is that, whenever you look at something, it's not merely an object you see. You're also seeing an entire chain of associations from the past, one that extends into the future as well. You could envision it as a virtual-reality simulation in which you click on the object with your gaze and all of your thoughts and feelings about it open out in a panoramic stream of memories and associations. You never really see this or any object for what it is. As *A Course in Miracles* states, "*I see only the past*"; "*I see nothing as it is now.*"[26]

Next, move on to another object. Again, it's better if you don't try to choose it consciously, but just allow your gaze to settle on it.

Repeat the inquiry above to unlock its past and future.

Then move on to the next object. Repeat this for at least three but no more than five objects, then stop. Close your eyes. Let go of all those memory chains. Click off of them, and shut down the thread from the past. Simply be still and at peace for as long as it's comfortable.

PART 2: SEEING WITHOUT NAMING

In chapter 1 we discussed your inner monologue, which poses as your *self* by providing a running commentary on your life. It makes judgments both positive and negative about you and everyone else as well. This voice has an opinion about everything, and it's not afraid to let you know what it thinks. But how could it play its judgment game if it were not able to attach a name to the things that make up your world?

A name is a convenient identifier. But it also reinforces separation. We pick out one sight or object from the background and, having given it a name, focus upon it. In the process, we exclude all other things with different names.

You have made up names for everything you see. Each one becomes a separate entity, identified by its own name. By this you carve it out of unity. By this you designate its special attributes, and set it off from other things by emphasizing space surrounding it. This space you lay between all things to which you give a different name; all happenings in terms of place and time; all bodies which are greeted by a name.

This space you see as setting off all things from one another is the means by which the world's perception is achieved. You see something where nothing is, and see as well nothing where there is unity.[27]

In this practice, we will attempt to look out on the world of perception, but without naming it. When we strip things of their names, we release them from the past. Without a name, we cannot identify the thing, and without an identifier, it can have no history, no past. Without the name, what is it really? Through this process, we knock out one of the main props holding up the ego's world of perception.

You'll find this practice somewhat similar to the last one in that it asks you to scan your environment and then select out certain objects at random. You can perform this indoors or outdoors, as you prefer. Let your eye settle on the object in question, then speak its name. You can do this in your mind or out loud, but either way be sure to say the name clearly. For example, you might say "door," "chair," "foot," "tree," "cloud," "window," or "photo."

After speaking its name, continue to stare at the object. Try to *see it* as it is, without any name. As you let go of the name, also let go of anything you think you know about this thing: its function, how it got there, whether you enjoy it or dislike it, and any other associations or judgments from the past. You see it fresh, unhampered by meaning, with beginner's mind.

Imagine that you've just landed in a spacecraft from another galaxy and that this object is the first thing you encounter on planet earth. You have no idea what it is. You are mystified. The best you can manage is to see its contours, colors, and its basic shape—but even these are vague, because you have no labels for round or square, tall or narrow, brown or green or blue. Stare at the object and try to reduce it to its essential *thingness*, stripped of all qualities, impressions, and descriptions. It is absent all context.

Be forewarned: this is not an easy practice. But that's the whole point—to discover just how tightly we're bound to the names and functions we've assigned these things. Each name ties us to a consensus reality which, without our awareness, has become very much a part of our self-concept. We never question it. As we noted, it also reinforces the "reality" of the inner voice that passes itself off as "us."

At the beginning, apply this practice to one or two objects at most. If it becomes too frustrating, stop. If, however, you're able to free yourself from names and functions for even an instant, you've accomplished something important. Either way, close your eyes and rest for a while before resuming your day.

You can repeat this procedure anytime and anywhere. With practice, you'll find that it becomes quite peaceful, because it helps to free you from Never-Mind. As you grow more comfortable with the process, you can apply it to as many different objects as you like.

PART 3: SEEING NO-THING

The last practice was an attempt to develop beginner's mind. You let go of everything you think you know in order to approach experience fresh, in the pure present, washed clean of past associations. It is possible to take this still further.

Earlier in the chapter, I described the plight of those born with congenital cataracts and how, even after cataract removal surgery, they were unable to see normally. They had never learned to identify objects as objects, much less give them names. In this practice, you will get a chance to try this radical embrace of beginner's mind for yourself.

Once again, sit comfortably and let your eyes scan the room or, if you're outside, the area immediately surrounding you. Imagine that you are one of those cataract patients suddenly able to perceive light and color for the first time, but not objects. As you look around, try to see shadings and contours, hues and textures, but without any sense of where one object ends and another begins. Obliterate all boundaries. Your visual field becomes a fluid wash of light and color, without objects, outlines, or sharp transitions of any kind. Then close your eyes and rest for a moment. Try it again.

DO NOT READ FURTHER
UNTIL YOU'VE COMPLETED THE PRACTICE.

OK, so how did that go for you? True confession: I have *never* been able to carry out this practice successfully. And I suspect that you were not able to either. It's almost impossible. I included it to demonstrate just how solid and unshakeable the world of perception has become for us. Once we've learned to *see* a world of distinct forms and objects *out there*, we can't *unsee* it. It's akin to trying to hear your native language as if it were foreign: nothing but a jumble of sounds without distinct words or meaning. Once you've learned to identify words, it's extremely difficult to go back and hear only sounds. There are other ways to work around this limit. Besides, this radical form of beginner's mind is not necessary for the Holy Spirit's plan for salvation.

PART 4: CONING DOWN PERCEPTION

You can perform this practice either sitting comfortably or lying down. If lying down, I'd recommend *not* doing it right before bed, as you're likely to fall asleep. Again, if you note any discomfort or anxiety, stop. But you're far more likely to experience the opposite: an unaccustomed sense of calmness and peace.

What you will be doing is to single out one thing and focus on it exclusively. Cone down your perceptual field, masking out all else if possible, such that only this single thing exists.

Traditionally, in meditative practice, the focus rests on the breath. So that is what we'll try first here. You will follow each breath, in and out, as it enters and leaves your nostrils. That point of contact between breath and nostrils becomes your universe—the only thing you know or have ever known. If other thoughts intrude or if your mind starts to wander, gently bring your focus back to the breath, as you might redirect a young child to a task they're reluctant to carry out. No judgment or coercion needed, just the reminder. This is something you want for yourself. But your Never-Mind will fight it. Patience and perseverance are necessary.

The breath is not the only option. There are other possible perceptions you can focus on. Staring into crackling flames in a fireplace or holding your gaze on a single, tiny candle flame will work just as well. As you stare at the flame(s), let go of all thoughts and impressions you've ever held about fire and flame and what they mean. You have never before encountered this kinetic dancing phenomenon of color, light, and heat, into which you now stare so intently. Let its *thingness* dissolve into an *isness*. Everything else fades away, first into irrelevance, then into nonexistence. This one thing you behold is all that exists. You and it are one.

This practice can work with a word as well. Choose any two- or three-syllable word and repeat it over and over to yourself, whether aloud or in your mind. Do not pause between repetitions. Speak the word in one continuous loop, doing your best not to alter your tone, your pace, or pronunciation. If your mind starts to wander, if other thoughts intrude, or if you stumble on a syllable and get thrown off, it doesn't matter. Just pick it back up and start repeating the word again.

If you can't think of a suitable word, psychologist Charles Tart used the word *cogitate*, which means to think deeply and intently about something. (I'm sure the irony was intentional.) He went so far as to record himself saying it over and over in an endless loop: *cog-i-tate, cog-i-tate, cog-i-tate, cog-i-tate,cog-i-tatecog-i-tatecog-i-tatecog-i-tatecog-i-tate* . . .

Notice how the word quickly loses any sense of meaning. It no longer represents whatever it once meant. Shortly after, its structure collapses. It's no longer a word at all, just an odd jumble of meaningless sounds. Where one begins and another ends is blurred beyond recognition. The sounds are purely nonsensical.

Put this book down and give it a try using any of the options just described. When you're done, come back and let's talk about what you've accomplished.

*   *   *

By focusing on your breath, a flame, or a word repetition, you confound the Never-Mind. You trip it up by depriving it of the context and contrast it depends upon, thereby robbing it of its ability to make interpretations and judgments. The result is a short-circuiting of the perceptual mechanism. In the all-encompassing·mental space created by your intense, one-pointed focus, all sense of the meaning of things, which you assigned to them, is gone, including your life story. Essentially, you've said "never mind" to the Never-Mind. You've eased it out of the way and allowed the doors of perception to swing open to the endless tranquility of Ever-Mind.

3

Touching Ever-Mind:
The Perfect Moment

In the first chapter, we dismantled the familiar ways in which you (or rather, your ego) define "self." This false self stands in the way of discovering your true Self. In chapter 2, we deconstructed the mechanisms behind perception in order to demonstrate that the world you *think* you see and live in—the one that seems to exist outside your body—is in actuality a construct of the Never-Mind. It cannot be considered real. Nor can anything that it offers you in the way of satisfaction be real or enduring.

At this point, then, you're probably a bit lost. You don't really know what you are or where you are. And if nothing is real, then what's the purpose of living?

In the midst of this uncertainty, it's time to offer a taste of something certain. We do not set about dismantling self and world for no reason. There is a purpose. So at this juncture, it will prove helpful to have some sense of what replaces them—a glimpse of the goal, a foretaste of the destination that awaits us.

Welcome to the perfect moment.

A Perfect Moment

Have you ever experienced a perfect moment? An interval of time during which you feel such a sense of peace, wonder, and beauty that nothing can disturb you? An instant in which time itself seems to pause and release its hold on you, past and future fall away, taking with them all anxieties, hurts and upsets? The very thought of them becomes laughably irrelevant. Nothing can disturb the peace of your being. And in the sparkling present that is now all that remains of time, the absolute perfection of everyone and everything reveals itself. Nothing is wrong, nothing out of place; all is for the best. As the fourteenth-century mystic Julian of Norwich wrote, "And all shall be well, and all manner of thing shall be well."[1]

I have been blessed with several such moments.

Hiking a sandy path along the shoreline of a remote fjord above the Arctic Circle in Norway, a brisk, steady wind, moist with salt spray, whipping off the choppy waters a mere thirty yards to my left. The path threads its way through a field of clover: thousands of tiny plants, their leaves gleaming bright emerald in the sunlight. Nestled within each plant, balanced perfectly at the juncture of its three leaves, sits a tiny bead of water condensed from the blowing sea spray. Each droplet catches the light of this eternal summer sun and reflects it back at me, winking. I walk through a field of scintillating scattered diamonds—stars fallen to grace the earth. I glance left and right, ahead, behind. Everywhere my gaze settles, a thousand pearls of light sparkle and daze me with their bright joyous laughter. My journey loses all sense of purpose. No goal, no endpoint. Only the insistent embrace of wind and sea commingled with the sparkling pinpoints of light. A perfect moment.

A warm day in spring. Seated on the New Haven Green, with a picnic lunch spread out on the manicured lawn to be shared among friends. The sky is an impossible shade of blue. A warm breeze wafts through my hair in a caress gentler than any mother's. Each individual blade of grass shines resplendent in the sunlight, as if lit from within. I brush my fingers across the tips of the luminous green blades, sifting them through my fingers as I might stroke the skin of a lover. And I know, with total conviction, that this moment is nothing less than Eden before the Fall. Perfection itself. A perfect moment.

Floating on my back atop a calm Appalachian lake at sunset, buoyed by a float resting just beneath my knees so that I am weightless, suspended, with no effort whatsoever on my part. The contours of my body dissolve into the water's liquid warmth. My face is cradled by a gentle circle of water that leaves only eyes, nose, and mouth exposed to the cooling mountain air. Above me, the clear purpling sky extends seemingly without limit, until it nips and kisses the water at the very edges of my vision. My breaths come slow and even—a gentle rolling motion—like the distant hills. I am sky and lake,

water and air, within and without—all one, all at peace. A
perfect moment.

One particularly powerful depiction of such a moment
comes towards the end of Eugene O'Neill's brilliant auto-
biographical play *Long Day's Journey Into Night*, the saga
of a family crippled by alcoholism and mental illness. The
youngest son, a sailor, has just heard his miserly, alcoholic
father admit to selling out for easy money when he could
have become a great Shakespearean actor—an unusually
sincere confession considering its source, full of regret and
dashed hopes. In return, the son shares with his father one
of his finest moments.

> *I was on the Squarehead, square rigger, bound for Bue-*
> *nos Aires. Full moon in the trades. The old hooker driving*
> *fourteen knots. I lay on the bowsprit, facing astern, with*
> *the water foaming into spume under me, the masts with*
> *every sail white in the moonlight, towering high above me.*
> *I became drunk with the beauty and singing rhythm of it,*
> *and for a moment I lost myself—actually lost my life. I was*
> *set free! I dissolved in the sea, became white sails and flying*
> *spray, became beauty and rhythm, became moonlight and*
> *the ship and the high dim-starred sky! I belonged, with-*
> *out past or future, within peace and unity and a wild joy,*
> *within something greater than my own life, or the life of*
> *Man, to Life itself! To God, if you want to put it that way.*[2]

Perfect moments such as these needn't last more than an instant, though they can play out over minutes or even hours.

Their duration is irrelevant, however, because once experienced, you can never again look at the world in quite the same way. You are changed. You've had a taste of something greater than your day-to-day self—of heaven on earth, one might say—a state of mind so radically apart from what you usually experience that, even when you return to the routine ordinariness of it all (or worse, to life's unanticipated trials and tragedies), you're no longer affected in the same way. You feel protected—swaddled in a peace that comes not from this world.

When the mirror of perception quietly shatters, when you pierce the veil of Never-Mind, this is the world you behold. You enter a perfect moment: the world seen through the eyes of Ever-Mind. *A Course in Miracles* calls this the *real world*. It rarely comes to us as a result of any particular event. Winning the big game, getting accepted to an Ivy League college, landing the deal of a lifetime, or finally hearing the words "I love you" from the lips of your beloved—these produce jubilation, triumph, relief perhaps, but as a rule they do not propel us into perfect moments.

French novelist Marcel Proust experienced a series of perfect moments throughout his life, each triggered, not by some event, but by a random, seemingly trivial perception: the taste of a soft cookie soaked in tea, the lines formed by the spires of a cathedral in the town of Martinville, stepping upon two uneven paving stones and momentarily losing balance. Can we honestly say that these were the *cause* of Proust's perfect moments? If so, then we would expect everyone to be compulsively dipping cookies in tea.

The Martinville cathedral would become a shrine to rival Lourdes.

The truth is, we don't know why such moments come to us when they do, other than the fact that Ever-Mind is always present, waiting in the wings, so to speak, for any opportunity we give it to step forth. After the fact, we make inferences about why this moment happened to occur. It was the linearity of cathedral spires, the sparkling pearls of light within the clover, the tossing of the ship on the waves in the moonlight. But this is the action of the ego trying to reassert itself and link the perfect moment to its world of things and events. It is also an attempt to retrace the path by which we arrived at the perfect moment, as if there were only one avenue leading there and we'd better not lose the directions. We try to preserve the moment, to etch it into memory and file it away, cataloged according to the circumstances that brought it about, like a museum specimen—some rainbow-winged dragonfly from a prehistoric era trapped forever in a block of amber. We pull up the memory on special occasions, view it in our minds, and sigh wistfully. Or we use it to bolster our unique sense of self, our specialness: "Let me tell you what happened to *me* one afternoon sitting on the New Haven Green!"

As a decades-long student of *A Course in Miracles*, I find that brief slices of perfect moments come my way often now. I need only pause and reflect that I have a choice, and then make the decision to shift from ego to Holy Spirit, from Never-Mind to Ever-Mind, from OS2 to OS1. The perfect moment has little to do with what is perceived out there in the world, because there *is* nothing *out there* to constitute a world. The perfect moment has everything to do with the *self,* the one that is doing the perceiving. Where Never-Mind sees objects, bodies, and events that busily shift and change, Ever-Mind beholds only perfection. It knows nothing else.

Now that I understand this, the truly puzzling question for me is, why do I still fall back into Never-Mind with such regularity? Why is it so easy to default to OS2 and forget there is another option? Why do we resist the call of Spirit when we know how good it feels? If there were a restaurant dishing up Ever-Mind or a church that offered it with the Sunday sermon, there would be lines around the block. People become addicted to heroin, alcohol, sex, food, high-risk sports, gambling—all of which result in a feeling of elation. Why don't we pursue our true Self with even a fraction of the same determination?

If the perfect moment is our best and most immediate example of Ever-Mind, then perhaps we would benefit by trying to understand it better.

Elements of the Perfect Moment

It seems almost silly to take an experience like the perfect moment, put it under a magnifying glass, and attempt to dissect it into its component parts. Wholeness cannot be grasped with the tools of fragmentation. But if we hope to understand such moments, then it will prove helpful to explore them more deeply.

What are the key elements that make up a perfect moment?

1. AN EXPANDED, EXPANSIVE SENSE OF SELF

Your sense of self expands beyond the familiar boundaries of your body. Even though the body remains present, it no longer confines you. Your identity soars outward, upward, transported beyond the body's cramped limits. Sensations like pain or hunger do not reach you in this state. In extreme cases, you lose all sense of a separate self. You feel at one with nature, all people, the whole universe, and God.

2. A PERVASIVE SENSE OF PEACEFULNESS

This is not the peace that comes from cessation of stress. This is not kicking off your shoes at the end of a long day or easing under the covers in anticipation of a good night's sleep. This peace does not arise from absence or relief. It is a positive force in its own right, which, by its very presence, pushes out anything that is not peaceful. It partners with an inner silence, pervasive and uninterruptable. That nattering voice in your head bows and stands aside for this silence—as if it had any choice. No earthly sound can compete with it, much less shatter it.

> *There is a silence into which the world can not intrude.*
> *There is an ancient peace you carry in your heart and have*
> *not lost.*[3]

This is the peace "which surpasses all understanding" mentioned in the Bible (Philippians 4:7, New Revised Standard Version), because it is not rational or comprehensible to the normal everyday mind. It is the peace of God.

3. AN EXPERIENCE OF LIGHT NOT OF THIS WORLD

We are naturally drawn to light. The full moon, iridescent neon signs, multicolored strings of Christmas bulbs, the shimmering aurora borealis—all call to us with an unearthly appeal. We see in them a reminder of our true nature. But the perfect moment dwarfs them all, bringing with it an experience of light like no other.

In the perfect moment, the things of this world appear suffused with light. This is not like regular light from a lightbulb or the sun's rays. It is an inner light, "*formless and without limit*,"[4] a light not so much seen with the eye as apprehended by the mind, which then interprets the experience as light. Surfaces are accentuated; objects are exposed as insubstantial, unreal, as if part of an elaborate hoax—a cleverly appointed stage set or museum diorama into which we happen to have wandered. And yet this light also bestows on the world a hyper-reality beyond anything we've known.

> *True light that makes vision possible is not the light the body's eyes behold. It is a state of mind that has become so unified that darkness cannot be perceived at all. And thus what is the same is seen as one, while what is not the same is unnoticed, for it is not there.*[5]

This light shines forth from people's faces as well. It is as if you peered right through the clumsy illusion of tissue and bone to a reality of absolute light that somehow filters through the flesh. And that light is ever so gentle. There is no need to turn away and hide your eyes. You want to clasp it, join with it, open yourself wide and take it in. It is light perceived not with the eyes, but with the heart. It is the visual equivalent of divine love. In its radiance, all beings are united.

> *There is a light that this world cannot give. Yet you can give it, as it was given you. And as you give it, it shines forth to call you from the world and follow it. For this light will attract you as nothing in this world can do. And you will lay aside the world and find another. This other world is bright with love. . . . Light is unlimited, and spreads across this world in quiet joy.*[6]

4. OVERWHELMING, UNCONDITIONAL LOVE

The love of the perfect moment is universal, like its light and peace. This love is what the ancient Greeks called *agape*. It is neither specific nor limited. It is not reserved for certain people and relationships, nor is it confined to particular circumstances, to the exclusion of others. It is literally overwhelming; it overflows all boundaries to encompass everyone and everything. If you met your worst enemy, you would feel nothing but love for him or her—because your mind has nothing but love to give. It is this love, in combination with the peace "which surpasses all understanding," that gives rise to the profound conviction that "all shall be well, and all manner of thing shall be well."

> *Love knows no bodies, and reaches to everything created like itself. Its total lack of limit is its meaning. It is completely*

impartial in its giving, encompassing only to preserve and
keep complete what it would give.[7]

Love is not like the things of this world. When you give it, you do not lose it. You gain. Both giver and receiver emerge with *more* love. According to *A Course in Miracles*, this property proves that love is not native to our world of bodies and things. It comes from God. The perfect moment confirms this. In its embrace, we give and receive simultaneously, intuitively knowing that there is no separation between giver and receiver: no one outside of us to give to or receive from. Love merely *is*, a given, an all-encompassing truth, a gift from the Self to Itself, and a reflection of the perfect love of God.

5. TOTAL ABSORPTION IN THE MOMENT

Time does not intrude on the perfect moment. It stands beyond time, in an eternal present. The past loses all relevance. One could go so far as to say it no longer exists. Certainly it no longer touches you. From the perspective of an eternal *now*, the very idea of a memory from the past seems flimsy and contrived. We recognize it for the illusion it is. And without the past, worries and fears are gone. Judgments are absent because, as we saw in the last chapter, judgment depends on past experience.

In the eternity of the perfect moment, you have no care for the future either: no anxiety, no desire; no yearnings or preferences for one outcome over another. You have complete trust in the unfolding of life. All is well, exactly as it should be. Perfect, in fact. You stand in full welcome of the present moment, whatever it may bring about. What else could you want? The very concept of wanting becomes absurd, because it implies a lack of some kind. Knowing that you lack nothing, that everything real and meaningful is already yours, you realize that there is no more wanting. You are incapable of it.

Recall that in the introduction we told the story of Goethe's Faust, a man who made a bargain with the devil in hopes of finding a moment in which he was so content with what is, so unconditionally happy, that he would wish the moment to last forever. What he sought was in fact what we are calling the perfect moment. But there's no need to wish that it last forever, because it already does. It is a timeless interval, liberated from the past, untethered from future concerns. It is nothing less than a window opening onto eternity.

6. A PROFOUND CONVICTION OF HOLINESS

The word *holy* is not one we use often. Not much strikes us as holy these days. Nor is holiness easy to define. Theologian Rudolf Otto wrote an entire book on the subject, *The Idea of the Holy*, yet still failed to nail it down. This is because holiness defies intellectual analysis. But we know it when we experience it.

No single religious tradition can lay claim to holiness. It transcends the doctrinal differences upon which the world's religions are established. The experience of holiness has nothing to do with your particular *beliefs* about God. Whether you practice as a Muslim, Jew, Christian, Hindu, Buddhist, or anything else, what is holy is holy.

Anything in this world can be holy—any object, structure, or place. Helen Schucman, scribe of *A Course in Miracles*, experienced profound holiness inside a dirty, smelly Manhattan subway car. Holiness lives within us, and it is bestowed by us. When we look on any aspect of the world with the vision of Ever-Mind, as we do in the perfect moment, then all is blessed. All is perfect. All is holy.

7. A SENSE OF PRESENCE

In the perfect moment, at one with the vastness of Ever-Mind, you feel yourself surrounded by something greater than yourself: a Presence vast, eternal and limitless, all-knowing and all-loving. It stands behind you protecting you. It goes before you smoothing your way. It hovers above you and around you. Some identify this Presence as God. For others, it's Jesus or Buddha or a guardian angel. I propose that it is the felt presence of Spirit, but experienced as if it were outside of and apart from you.

However we understand it, the feeling is one of complete safety, absolute love, and unerring guidance. It's the feeling a frightened child has when she senses herself uplifted into the arms of a loving mother who will carry her through whatever perils she feared. Or, as the Bible puts it, "Yea, though I walk through the valley of the shadow of death, I will fear no evil: for thou art with me" (Psalm 23:4, King James Version).

Bill Wilson, founder of Alcoholics Anonymous, experienced this sense of Presence at several points in his life. While a patient at Townsend Hospital, where he was trying to recover from alcoholism, he described it as "the fresh clean wind of a mountain top blowing thru and thru me."[8] The experience inspired him to found Alcoholics Anonymous, based (initially) on the idea that transformative experience can cure addiction. Millions have benefitted from his encounters with the perfect moment.

* * *

A Course in Miracles, in its Clarification of Terms, clearly states that the goal of its teaching is not theoretical or scholarly, but experiential and practical: a universal experience of truth, love and oneness. The perfect moment is such an experience. Here is the Course's explanation for what happens in the perfect moment.

> *Everyone has experienced what he would call a sense of being transported beyond himself. . . . It is a sense of actual escape from limitations. If you will consider what this "transportation" really entails, you will realize that it is a sudden unawareness of the body, and a joining of yourself and something else in which your mind enlarges to encompass it. It becomes part of you, as you unite with it. And both become whole, as neither is perceived as separate. What really happens is that you have given up the illusion of a limited awareness, and lost your fear of union. The love that instantly replaces it extends to what has freed you, and unites with it. And while this lasts you are not uncertain of your Identity, and would not limit It. You have escaped from fear to peace, asking no questions of reality, but merely accepting it. You have accepted this instead of the body, and have let yourself be one with something beyond it, simply by not letting your mind be limited by it.*[9]

In the perfect moment, we drop our limited awareness of a self that's identified with a body and instead embrace union with something greater. It is our willingness to join with this something greater that reawakens us to the presence of Spirit and floods us with its light, peace, love, and holiness, all in one expansive, eternal present moment. We receive a taste of the Course's *real world*.

Stumbling into Perfect Moments

How do perfect moments come about? Obviously they cannot be engineered. Rather, we seem to stumble into them, often when we're least expecting it. As we mentioned, the external prompts that trigger the experience are mere window dressing—the Never-Mind's attempt to make sense of the experience after the fact and anchor it firmly in its own world. Nevertheless, there are some commonalities in how perfect moments arise that are worth noting, if only because they all point away from ego toward Spirit.

1. NATURE

Nature plays an outsize role in catalyzing perfect moments. The sheer vastness of sky and sea brings us face-to-face with the infinite and seems to invite such moments. When we behold a majestic panorama—whether from the heights of a mountain top, a cliff side, a hot-air balloon, or outer space—our ego identity begins to break up, leaving our mind free to merge with the vast, open spaciousness. (One famous example was Apollo 14 astronaut Edgar Mitchell, who entered an expansive mystical state when he looked

upon the blue-white orb of the earth from his space cap-
sule.) It is as if the broadening of our visual horizons called
us to similarly broaden and release the boundaries of self.

Staring into the flickering flames of a fire, gazing at
swirling patterns in storm clouds, or tracking the contours
of sheets of rain as it curtains across the surface of a lake,
all can lift us out of our customary mindset into an expansive state. When the senses attempt to take in such infinite
patterning and variation, they rapidly grow overwhelmed.
Words fail, categories implode, thoughts dwindle to still-
ness, and we are left with something pure and calm and
beautiful.

In the practices for chapter 2, we saw how we could
circumvent the perceptual lockdown of the Never-Mind by
focusing in on a single, simple percept: a candle flame, a
repeated word, the rhythm of the breath. We achieve the
same result when we expand the perceptual field outward
to the point where Never-Mind is so flooded with input
that it's overwhelmed and has to let go. In either direction,
context and contrast collapse. The world of differences slips
away into unity and we can no longer sustain the illusion
of a separate, individual self.

2. PSYCHEDELIC DRUGS

Psychedelic drugs are famous for altering the mind by jar-
ring loose its accustomed grip on "reality." In the previous
chapter, we mentioned writer Aldous Huxley, whose book
The Doors of Perception described in detail a transcendent
experience with the drug mescaline (derived from the pey-
ote cactus). Back in the 1960s, Harvard professor Timothy

Leary popularized LSD and the acid trip. More recently, Western shaman Alberto Villoldo, PhD and psychologist Rachel Harris, PhD have related their encounters with the increasingly popular psychedelic beverage ayahuasca produced in the Amazon.

Psychedelics do indeed alter the sense of self. They accomplish this by undermining the familiar perceptual framework on which the Never-Mind depends for its existence. If the world turns out not to be what you thought—if, under the action of a psychedelic, its component parts literally melt out from under you—then how can you perpetuate the charade that it's substantial and real? And if the world is unreal, then what does that say about *you,* who sheltered within its illusions with such certainty?

Psychedelics knock out the moorings that prop up the self-concept. They cut through custom and memory to flay the mind and lay it bare to a new reality. But the flaying process can be painful and scary; it risks damaging the mind. Preparation and expert guidance are necessary to ensure a "good trip."

3. EXTREME PHYSICAL EXERTION

Extreme physical exertion will sometimes induce expanded, ecstatic awareness. Runners, swimmers, dancers, and other athletes report finding themselves in a state of perfect flow when, as a result of training, they no longer need to consciously focus on what their body is doing and instead lose themselves—and their sense of self—in its motion. The whirling dervishes of Sufism disrupt the senses to enter ecstatic states through incessant spinning. I have witnessed the same spinning phenomenon among fans of the rock band The Grateful Dead at their concerts.

4. ILLNESS OR CLINICAL DEATH

Severe illness or a brush with death (the near-death experience) can spark the awareness that consciousness is not restricted to the physical body, but extends well beyond it. This has been well-documented in many popular books. The reason for it is obvious. When seriously ill or dying, the ego must let go and consciousness sails free.

5. SEXUAL CLIMAX

Perhaps the most widely experienced, though least discussed, trigger for expanded awareness is the ecstasy of sexual orgasm, which has the potential to kick the mind into an intense, but all-too-brief, state of expansion, union, and peacefulness that teeters at the edges of losing consciousness. The French label this *la petite mort* or "the little death." As with the near-death experience and extreme physical exertion, the body's intense arousal allows us, rather ironically, to transcend its limits. But it also pulls us back, and does so rather quickly. I will have more to say about sexuality and orgasm in relation to *A Course in Miracles* in a later book in this series.

*   *   *

Unfortunately, none of these pathways can be counted upon to bring about the perfect moment. People frequently gaze out over scenic vistas, run marathons, have near-brushes with death, and engage in sex, all without the slightest hint of a perfect moment. Such moments can't be consciously orchestrated or compelled. Indeed the attempt to do so will most likely backfire and subvert the very goal it seeks.

Not even psychedelics can guarantee perfect moments. On the contrary, ask anyone who's white-knuckled their way through a bad trip. Ecstatic expansion all too easily flips into nightmarish contraction under the influence of psychoactive substances, especially if the setting does not feel safe and supportive.

However much we may wish for it, there is no magic formula for inducing perfect moments. And for all but a rare few, these moments do not last. They do not open into full, ongoing enlightenment. Our struggles with work, money, relationships, and health steal back into our minds, usually without much conscious awareness. That wonderful instant when we knew with absolute certainty that "all shall be well" hardens into memory. We haul it out on occasion and recall it fondly, like a faded photo from a happy occasion, but its ability to move us grows increasingly remote. And perhaps this is inevitable. How could we possibly function in day-to-day life if we looked on all things from a perch of infinite peace, love, and light?

But if the moment *could* last, if you could enter such deep states of beauty, peace and joy and sustain them, would you want that?

Losing the Moment

According to *A Course in Miracles* and mystics of all traditions, the goal of the spiritual journey is enlightenment, salvation, awakening from the ego's nightmare to the perfection of light, love, peace, timelessness, holiness, and presence. This experience is far closer to reality—the *real world* that the Course describes—than the fleeting interval between birth and death that we label life. Ever-Mind is with us always, only we fail to recognize it, much less embrace it. We actively push it away. We've got better things to do with our time, more urgent matters to attend to.

Had I walked through that field of clover in Norway wearing dark, polarized sunglasses, I would have missed the ten thousand pearls of light glistening within the leaves of clover. The thoughts of Never-Mind are like the darkest of sunglasses; they blind us to the perfection inherent in each moment. Had I set out on my hike along that Norwegian fjord already angry over some insult, or fearful I was trespassing and might get arrested, or fretting about how I would pay for my return flight to the United States, I would have missed the whole thing. Had I been intent on reaching the end of the trail in order to sleep, eat, or meet up with my girlfriend, or had I been racing to get there in record time, ahead of all others—that is, had I pursued some goal tied to my body's needs or my personal identity—the perfect moment would have eluded me. I would probably have taken note of the sparkling droplets in the clover, perhaps even marveled at their beauty, but only as an afterthought. They would not have freed my mind to enter an eternal present. My focus on the past and future would have kept me earthbound.

To the extent that you continue to embrace the narrow self-concept that is Never-Mind, the perfect moment will strike you as an anomaly. Nice if it happens, but let's get real. Don't expect it. Besides, you have more important things to worry about. How secure is your job? How solid is your marriage? How reliable is your health-care plan? How hefty is your retirement fund? These are what matter. And why bother chasing after perfect moments when you have the old reliable standbys of sex, drugs, and rock 'n' roll to get you through the night?

Recall the man searching for his keys under the streetlamp from chapter 1? We learned that we are more like him than we care to admit. Unlike that man, however, we search not in light, but in darkness, because we have confused darkness and light. Figuratively, we've been told that light comes from streetlamps and nowhere else. Their dim glow is our only source of clarity, our only hope for finding our way. We accept this as true and bravely make the best of it. The perfect moment offers a vision of real light amidst this darkness, as if the sun had emerged in all its splendor, however briefly, and exposed the folly of our situation—that we've been groping about in darkness. The perfect moment illuminates a state of mind so different from what we label normal that we would welcome it and rest there forever, if only we could. And perhaps we can—if we trust its certainty over that of the Never-Mind and did not at some point drop to our knees and begin once again pawing at the ground, in the darkness, expecting to find something that does not exist where we look for it.

The single greatest impediment to the perfect moment is your identification with the ego. In fact, without the ego there is only perfection: the still, calm perfection of Spirit, in which "all manner of thing shall be well." Therefore the only way to access perfect moments more consistently and reliably is to learn to recognize ego in all of its many guises and let it go. A core theme of the Course and of this book—one we will revisit frequently—is that if you want to achieve abiding inner peace, you must first eliminate all that is not peaceful.

A Course in Miracles is very clear that it is a course in *undoing*, in "removing the blocks to the awareness of love's presence, which is your natural inheritance."[10] You cannot get to Ever-Mind without unlearning the habits of Never-Mind. You cannot hear the quiet voice of the Holy Spirit if your allegiance remains tied to the ego's empty inner monologue. You cannot feel the sun's warmth or inhale the freshness of the breeze if you insist on staying in your prison cell, and ignore the wide-open door, because you are convinced that nothing worthwhile lies beyond it. You must abandon your hollow conviction that you *know* what is best, what is real, and make a different choice if you are to find your real home in God. It's your only option.

Vision: Seeing Oneness in All Things

A Course in Miracles makes use of many different concepts and metaphors to bring us to the realization of our true nature: our oneness with God and with each other. However, there is one concept that runs throughout the Text and Workbook more consistently than any other—even more than forgiveness or miracles. The Course returns to it again and again. It is the concept of vision, or more specifically, Christ's vision. Recall that the word *Christ* in *A Course in Miracles* does not refer to the person of Jesus of Nazareth, although it does refer to the Son of God. Let me explain. The Course, dictated to Dr. Helen Schucman by an inner Voice she identified as Jesus, explains that we are *all*, collectively, God's Son. The Course uses the masculine *Son* partly because of the era in which it was written, but more in an attempt to redefine the term and free it from the meaning it was given in Christianity, which identifies it exclusively with Jesus. Jesus was not unique; he simply awoke to his true nature ahead of the rest of us and tried to teach us what he'd learned—that we are *all* aspects of the one Son of God; we are God's offspring, the extension of God's limitless Being, which is love and nothing but love.

Christ's vision then is the vision that *sees only Christ*—only oneness, only God, only love—in all people and things. It is simultaneously the vision that we use once we awaken to the fact that we too are Christ. The Christ in us looks out and beholds the Christ in everyone else. It is the ultimate recognition that we are not bodies, but mind, and that mind is one.

> *Christ's vision has one law. It does not look upon a body, and mistake it for the Son whom God created. It beholds a light beyond the body; an idea beyond what can be touched; a purity undimmed by errors, pitiful mistakes, and fearful thoughts. . . . And it looks on everyone, on every circumstance, all happenings and all events, without the slightest fading of the light it sees.*[11]

When we look with Christ's vision to behold God in all things, we *undo* the differences on which perception rests. We literally overlook them and reinstate the truth of God's Creation.

> *Learn how to look on all things with love, appreciation and open-mindedness. You do not see them now. Would you know what is in them? Nothing is as it appears to you. Its holy purpose stands beyond your little range.*[12]

In the perfect moment, then, we see not with the body's eyes, but with the "eyes" of love. Using Christ's vision, we peer past the ego's world of perception—past division, past contrast—and heal these splits by recognizing our fundamental oneness with all that exists. Workbook Lesson 30 states: "*God is in everything I see because God is in my mind.*" It goes on to describe this idea as "the springboard for vision."

> *We are trying to see in the world what is in our minds, and what we want to recognize is there. Thus, we are trying to join with what we see, rather than keeping it apart from us. That is the fundamental difference between vision and the way you see. . . . Real vision is not limited to concepts such as "near" and "far." It does not depend on the body's eyes at all. The mind is its only source.*[13]

We join with what we see, because it is all a product of the mind. Thus, it is not so much a joining as a rejoining. As in *Through the Looking Glass*, we invert the false mirror of perception and peer through the illusion to behold the *real world*, that is, the world purified of all the grime and distortions introduced by the ego-mind. Recall the quote from earlier in this chapter about being transported beyond yourself:

> *What really happens is that you have given up the illusion of a limited awareness, and lost your fear of union. The love that instantly replaces it extends to what has freed you, and unites with it. And while this lasts you are not uncertain of your Identity, and would not limit It.*[14]

In the perfect moment, we sample true vision. We look upon infinite, all-loving oneness and recognize it for what it is: nothing less than our true Self—the Self as God created it.

PRACTICE

If Ever-Mind is always present and available to us, then why are perfect moments so rare? And why are we willing to accept that? How can we scoff and pretend that they're not all that important? Imagine how it would feel to know that once a day (once a month even) you were guaranteed a perfect moment? How might it change your sense of things to know that complete freedom from worry and strife could be yours on a regular basis? This very moment your mind could open into a perfect moment. But you must choose it. And that's not possible if your mind is preoccupied with the junk thoughts of Never-Mind. You must clear these first to make room for the perfect moment.

In this practice, you are not going to chase after the perfect moment. That will not work. Instead you will begin to look at all that clogs your mind and keeps the perfect moment from flowing to you.

Start by asking yourself if you're *willing* to have a perfect moment. If a saint or guru were to materialize before you and, with a radiant smile, offer you just such a moment *right now*, would you accept it?

If you answered with an unequivocal *yes*, then bravo! But complete the practice anyway.

If you answered no, however, then why not? Would you prefer it come later, at a more convenient time? Why? The answer can only be that there are things you consider more important. Or are you afraid of it and would reject it anytime, anywhere? If so, look honestly at your fear and simply acknowledge it to yourself.

We will now try to inventory the kinds of thoughts that the ego throws at us to block the experience of holiness in the perfect moment. Then you will at least have a choice about whether you want to hold on to them or begin to let them go.

- Work or school demands
- Parenting responsibilities: school, health, safety
- Householder chores: grocery shopping, preparing meals, cleaning, arranging for repairs and maintenance, paying bills, yard work
- Concerns about appearances: how you look, dress, and present yourself; how you think others see you; keeping fit and attractive (working out, hairstyles, etc.)
- Upcoming appointments to be remembered
- Past failures and things you regret; things you did or did not do to your satisfaction; anything about which you regularly feel guilt or shame
- Pleasurable activities: things you look forward to, like eating out, snacking, drinking or drugging, sex, playing sports, or even that TV series that has you hooked
- Possessions you want or hope to purchase, like cars, clothing, shoes, jewelry, antiques, music, dream homes
- Experiences you want to have, like travel, beach vacations, concerts, sports events
- Longer-term worries like health, relationships, the well-being of those you love, financial security, retirement, and ultimately death.

*   *   *

Note how many different options the ego has for sidetracking you from your purpose. Observe which of the above are its favorites, its reliable standbys, when it tries to yank you out of peace and back into its arms, like some tiresome old lover who is jealous at the thought that you might actually find happiness apart from them.

Recall Julian of Norwich's "All shall be well, and all manner of thing shall be well." What if this were true for you? Workbook Lesson 292 promises: *"A happy outcome to all things is sure."* Assume for the moment that this is the case (though probably not in the way you picture it). How many times have you worked yourself into a frenzy over something that turned out to be no big deal, something that pretty much resolved itself? And even the bigger, thornier problems, when viewed years later with the benefit of hindsight, provoke no more than a gentle sigh or quiet chuckle. Now apply that insight to all of the concerns and desires you identified from the list that haunt you today. And then remember, a happy outcome is sure!

Let's return to the perfect moment. Workbook Lessons 101 and 102 tell us, *"God's Will for me is perfect happiness"* and *"I share God's Will for happiness for me."* If this is so, then you have every right to call upon the perfect moment and make it yours—not out of desperation or some need to be more special and holy than anyone else, but because it is your birthright and you are ready to claim it.

Do so. Now.

And then be patient. Let the Holy Spirit decide which circumstances are best suited to open your mind to a perfect moment. Trust Him. And remain vigilant for the ego's cunning attempts to pull you back into fear. And then trust Him again to help you find your way past the ego. When the time is right, you will stumble into that perfect moment. And all shall be well.

4

The Call of Wholeness

Spring, 1983. I had been living in Philadelphia for over five years, plenty long enough to join the city's base of impassioned sports fans. The Phillies had won the World Series in 1980 and now it looked like the 76ers had a shot at the N.B.A. title for the first time in almost twenty years. I was a huge fan in particular of Julius Erving, a gracious, soft-spoken power forward who with his gravity-defying twists and spins had changed the way basketball would be played forever. He of all people *deserved* to win a title. The Sixers swept through the playoffs like a swarm of locusts, devouring every opponent, losing only one game. In the N.B.A. finals, they beat Magic Johnson's L.A. Lakers in four straight games: a clean sweep.

Like many American cities in the 1980s, Philadelphia was riven by racial tension. Two years after the Sixers swept the Lakers, police burned an entire African-American neighborhood to the ground in order to flush out an African-American liberation group known as M.O.V.E. But on the night when the Sixers took the N.B.A. crown, none of that was to be seen.

I was living with my fiancée at the time. She did not understand how anyone could get so worked up over a stupid sporting event. Needless to say, she was not inclined to share my celebratory mood. But I *needed* to share it. So I got in my car and drove to City Line Avenue, the boundary between the inner city and the wealthier suburbs known as the Main Line (made famous by Katharine Hepburn and Cary Grant in the movie *The Philadelphia Story*.) The four-lane thoroughfare was crowded. Horns blared. Groups of men, mostly African-American, stood along the center line in the middle of the road. They brandished brooms, symbolic of the Sixers' sweep of the Lakers. I drove slowly by in the left lane, my left hand extended out the window, slapping high-fives with one after another after another of the broom sweepers as we laughed and shouted together in our jubilation. Under normal circumstances, our lives would not have crossed. Or if they had, we likely would have viewed each other through the characteristic lenses of racial and cultural bias. But not on this night. On this night, we were one: one people, one city, unified in our team's triumph.

Such celebrations are hardly a rarity. When teams like the Boston Red Sox or Chicago Cubs ended their nearly century-long droughts to finally win World Series titles, the jubilation lasted for days. How much more so with the massive crowds that turned out for the VE and VJ Day parades at end of World War II! When we join in such a collective outpouring of joy, the feeling is overwhelming. The event itself may occupy only a few hours, but the remembrance lasts a lifetime.

Lessons from Geese

Let's turn now from happy, cheering throngs to a quieter scene: a flock of Canadian geese migrating south for the winter. They fly in a graceful V-formation, silhouetted against the deep blue sky. The lead position shifts from goose to goose over the duration of the journey. They recognize landmarks below and navigate instinctively to the location where they'll be resting for the night, exactly as they've done for years and will continue to do for years to come. They know their final destination as well.

What could a flock of geese and jubilant Philadelphia sports fans possibly have in common? One is a frenzied, disorderly gathering in which random strangers come together to celebrate a special set of circumstances that may not recur for decades. The other is an orderly, patterned affair, as predictable as the procession of the seasons that give rise to it.

The answer? In both, the individual has willingly joined with others and merged its identity with that of a larger group which, for a time, imparts a wider sense of meaning and purpose. Meaning and purpose differ for each group, of course. The geese want to reach their winter home. They are practiced in their route and roles; they'd better be if they hope to escape the cold. The Sixers' fans, by contrast, have no meaning or purpose outside celebrating. Yet the sheer spontaneity of that celebration, the enormity of an entire city springing up from its couches and TV sets with a shout at the exact same moment and taking to the streets—not in protest or fear, but coming together in glee; dissolving boundaries of class, culture and race for one night—that is a rare and wonderful thing to behold.

The geese are hardly unique. There are many examples of this sort of collaboration in the animal kingdom. Ants work diligently to build vast underground colonies; termites construct huge, tunnel-filled mounds, the equivalent of a human city crisscrossed with streets; bees scout pollen-laden blossoms and convey their locations to fellow workers through complicated flying dances, all for the good of the hive. These collective endeavors are driven, like the geese, by the need of these organisms to survive, and thrive.

Humans in hunter-gatherer societies must bond for survival as well. They naturally unite to form tribal societies that extend well beyond typical family ties. The tribe is, for its members, the entire world. They rely on each other to meet all possible needs: food, shelter, parenting, sex, entertainment, healing, and ritual. Similarly, immigrants will settle in the same neighborhoods for safety, and to preserve common cultural traditions in their new and unfamiliar surroundings. My grandfather Arthur lived just across the street from his younger brother's family. My grandmother, Arthur's wife, lived three doors down from her younger sister, while her older sister lived across the street. Not exactly a tribe, but more than what most of us think of today as family.

Throughout nature we find this imperative to come together, to join with others of our kind. And yet, in saying this, I betray a certain bias—one we all hold—namely, the ego's penchant for separation over wholeness. Let me explain.

In the first chapter, we explored the way that physical bodies and private minds contribute to a unique sense of self, and how this loosely constructed patchwork of an identity turns out to rest upon some very shaky ground. In chapter 2, we saw how perception itself divides the world into separate objects and discrete events. To the extent that we see ourselves as individuals living in such a world, we will view our fellow inhabitants with the same bias. We see others as individuals like ourselves—isolated minds housed in separate bodies. As *A Course in Miracles* puts it:

> *Everyone makes an ego or a self for himself, which is subject to enormous variation because of its instability. He also makes an ego for everyone else he perceives, which is equally variable.*[1]

We populate our world with these myriad separate egos. We assign motives to their actions, which we base on our own motives. We make judgments; we approve or reject. And we affiliate in groups. But no matter how many groups we form with other egos or how strong our loyalty to them may be, they rarely override our most fundamental sense of self. We remain individuals who happen to have chosen to belong to a group. But the fact that we view groups with this bias doesn't make it true, any more than the ego itself is a true reflection of who we are.

What exactly is this balancing act between individual and group identity? How much of who we are is centered on our individuality and how much in the greater social group? Certainly, when I took that drive down City Line Avenue, slapping giddy high-fives with random strangers, I did not forget my identity: my job, my house, my fiancée. In fact, much of the joy of the experience came from knowing that, despite our dissimilar lives and backgrounds, I could gather with these strangers and embrace our shared group identity as triumphant Sixers fans.

For the geese, I suspect the opposite is true; their group identity overshadows the individual. Would an individual goose ever attempt to make the migratory journey flying solo? Would the group allow itself to be diverted from its flight path by the needs or wishes of its individual members? Likewise, could any ant, bee, or termite possibly exist on its own? Would the concept of "on its own" even make sense to them?

In Whole or in Parts

It is worth asking, then: Which is the actual organism, the goose or the flock? The bee or the hive? The ant or the colony? Where we see individual organisms working together toward a common goal, we could just as easily see one single entity with many loosely coordinated, component parts. Perhaps the hive, the colony, or the termite mound is the real organism. This viewpoint may sound strange, but only because it forces you to think of your separate self as one of those component parts, and your ego takes umbrage at any idea that diminishes its stature. But belonging to a group can have a profound effect on behavior. Quite simply, groups achieve things that individuals cannot. This is true in nature with bees and ants, obviously, but it is equally the case for humans.

Steve Jobs and Steve Wozniak could tinker in their garage to come up with the design for a personal computer, but it required a vast organization to design, manufacture, and distribute the array of products that today carry the Apple logo and that have changed the way we interconnect as humans. This was as true in the past as it is today. No single human could have built the pyramids of Egypt and Meso-America, the Great Wall of China, the monolithic stone circles of Great Britain, the medieval cathedrals of Europe, or the giant carved faces staring seaward from the heights of Rapa Nui. The effort of hundreds, maybe thousands, of workers, toiling anonymously over entire lifetimes was necessary—proof of the power of an organized group with a shared purpose.

Groups have a darker side as well. An unruly mob can wreak devastation, destroying property and even taking lives with no hesitation or remorse. Political movements like the Nazis in World War II, Pol Pot and his Khmer Rouge in Cambodia, or the Spanish Inquisition have inflicted violence, death, and outright genocide on a scale no serial killer could ever hope to match by himself. Yet whether the outcome of group behavior is positive or negative, we cannot downplay its power or its ability to attract and draw us in.

Groups are compelling. We *want* to join, to become a part of something bigger, whether that's a high-school football team or a presidential campaign. We want to strive towards a higher purpose. We want to give our lives over to the kind of meaning that comes only from dedication to an ideal greater than our individual self. And the more who share our cause, the more compelling it becomes. Why else would so many be willing to risk death in service to their country? However, this also explains how terrorist groups can attract converts from all over the world. They tempt those who have lost their homelands and who are starved for meaning with the promise of enlisting in a grand, noble cause, one worth fighting for, even dying for. Better a glorious death than a shabby, inconsequential life, impoverished and jobless, on the streets of some pitiless, indifferent city.

Cults and Tribes

Let's look now at two very similar types of group affiliation, each of which demonstrates the power of belonging to something greater than oneself, but with very different outcomes: cults and tribes. Cults coalesce around charismatic figures who claim to have special knowledge, power, or influence, usually due to their supposed direct and privileged connection to the divine. The leader's words are considered absolute truth; no one dares question them. The leader's exalted status is conferred upon him by God and it extends to his or her followers so long as they blindly obey the leader's dictates, even if this involves breaking the law or hurting others.

Cult members are encouraged to abandon their former lives by severing all ties with noncult family, friends, and careers in order to fully embrace the superior life of the cult. Sometimes the leader gives them new names to reinforce their new identities. Any attempts to leave are met with harsh rebuke and even punishment. This is necessary, because leaving the cult implies a challenge to the leader's authority. If members were permitted to leave with impunity, then others might also come to question the value of whatever doctrine the leader happens to be peddling and leave as well. As a result, the cult must enforce cohesion by crushing even the most minor challenges to the leader's authority. The leader, along with his or her closest lieutenants, must control cult members and coerce them into obedience to rigid cult norms.

Death is preferable to leaving. Indeed, many cults harbor a secret longing for death, which they frame as the ultimate release from and triumph over the bonds of the sordid external world. The People's Temple (at Jonestown), Heaven's Gate, and the Branch Davidians were all examples of cults that ended in the mass extermination of their memberships.

Given so many negatives, you might wonder why cults continue to exist. What's their appeal? The cult imparts to its members a sense of meaning and purpose that eluded them in normal life. The cult renders them special—not as individuals, not because of anything they've accomplished, but simply by virtue of belonging to such a privileged group. The cult masquerades as the ideal family, its leader as the ideal parent, showering acceptance upon its members in return for their unquestioning loyalty. The price of belonging—namely, giving up their personal identities—seems well worth the trade-off.

*   *   *

When we think of the pioneers who settled the West and Midwest of the United States, the image that first comes to mind is that of the rugged backwoodsman: Daniel Boone with his coonskin cap and sheathed hunting knife, gripping his flintlock rifle as he scouts the woods for game and danger, or mountain man Jeremiah Johnson (from the movie of the same name), contending with all measure of hardship in order to survive on his own. But solo survival was a rarity—perhaps an impossibility. The American veneration of the stalwart individual who conquers whatever perils come his way once again betrays our bias toward valuing individuality over the group. The more common, and far more successful, means of addressing the survival challenges posed by the forests and Great Plains of America was banding together in tribal groups.

At first glance, tribes and cults look similar. Both involve groups of people living in close proximity, united by a shared social identity and purpose. Both have rules, mores, and taboos that must not be broken. Both have leaders. But the cult comes into being primarily because of the leader's powerful personality and seemingly unique brand of wisdom that attracts converts. Its organizational structure is top-down. The leader determines everything. Should the leader die, the cult becomes rudderless until a new leader takes charge.

Tribes on the other hand are organized from the bottom up. Leaders arise from the members themselves, chosen by the tribe for their experience, wisdom, and courage. In other words, they've already proven themselves. They serve the interests of the tribe, not their own egos. Like the geese, bees and ants, the tribe is all about survival—not of the individual, but the collective. Any individual life is expendable if necessary, even that of the chief, because the tribe is the organism that must survive. The individual is merely a part that serves the whole.

Modern society offers little to help us understand the immense appeal of tribal life. Who today would choose to give up their house, job, family, and all the benefits of civilization to join a tribal society? In my celebration of the Sixers' championship, I gladly fraternized with the broom-sweeping revelers. But once the excitement died down, I returned home, watched the news on TV, and went to bed. The next day, I drove to work as usual. Nothing had changed as far as my sense of self was concerned. Even for soldiers in the same combat unit—as close a bond as any in the modern world—once the fighting is over, they return home to their separate lives. They shared the experience of battle and became a "band of brothers," but even this does not eclipse their individual identities.

Sebastian Junger in his 2016 book *Tribe* paints a vivid picture of the appeal of tribal life, not only for the American Indians, but for the European settlers of the seventeenth and eighteenth centuries as well. He does this, not so much by taking us inside the inner workings of the tribal camp, but by contrasting it with the unappealing nature of Western so-called civilization. (Any number of popular movies have undertaken this as well, including *Little Big Man* and *Dances with Wolves*.) But what's most striking about Junger's account are the contemporaneous, eyewitness statements testifying to the power of this appeal.

No less a light than Ben Franklin pointed out that "there were numerous settlers who were captured [by Indians] as adults and still seemed to prefer Indian society to their own."[2] Indeed, many settlers who were captured, then rescued and returned to their original families, chose to break free and escape back to their adopted tribal families. Junger quotes a French émigré who observed, "Thousands of Europeans are Indians, and we have no examples of even one of those Aborigines having from choice become European. There must be in their social bond something singularly captivating and far superior to anything to be boasted of among us."[3]

For women in particular, the egalitarian nature of tribal society offered a welcome relief from the strictures of civilization. Junger quotes one anonymous woman speaking of her life within the tribe: "Here I have no master. I am the equal of all the women in the tribe, I do what I please without anyone's saying anything about it, I work only for myself, I shall marry if I wish and be unmarried again when I wish. Is there [any] woman as independent as I in your cities?"[4] Neither the English Puritans, French trappers, or Spanish conquerors held women in such regard.

Perhaps because of the highly egalitarian nature of tribal society, the notion of treason was unheard of. No member would ever think of betraying the tribe that nurtured and protected his life. Loyalty came without question; unlike the cult, it needed no enforcement.

Tribal members take on the communal identity of the tribe, and having done so, they choose never to abandon that identity, even when forcibly abducted from the tribe and returned to civilization. Quite a contrast to the world of the cult, where control over group members and their lives is absolute and top-down, and those attempting to leave are subject to harsh punishment. What gives rise to such a profound difference?

The Power of Shared Purpose

A Course in Miracles tells us that the first step on the path back to unity is the recognition, in one form or another, that your interests are identical to those of someone else. "*Only a purpose unifies, and those who share a purpose have a mind as one.*"[5] This can be as simple as playing on the same Little League team or as intense as embarking on a clandestine Special Forces combat mission. For that interval of time, your purpose on earth is the same.

> *When two minds join as one and share one idea equally, the first link in the awareness [that all minds are] one has been made.*[6]

Both cults and tribes offer their members an opportunity to embrace this shared sense of purpose—which is the reason for their powerful appeal. But because the cult is organized around the personality of its leader with all his quirks and whims, this joining together in a common purpose must be unstable. The leader is very much a flawed human being, no different really from any of his followers. As he shifts and turns, reacting and overreacting, picking favorites and picking on outcasts, the shared purpose of the cult begins to fray. Eventually it falls apart, because it was not anchored in the bedrock of truth. The sense of unity it conferred was capricious and transitory, and therefore false. It was a unity derived from a single individual, a group identity fashioned on and amplified by the persona of the leader.

The bottom-up organization of the tribe leads to much greater stability. Because the leader serves the tribe and all its members equally, her decisions tend to bring the group together rather than splitting it into competing factions. Within the oneness of the tribal group, there is room for differences; in fact, these are not just tolerated, but welcomed and valued. Thus there is less need to enforce conformity through top-down control.

But there is another, far bigger difference between tribes and cults—one that helps explain why cult members so frequently try to escape, while tribal members resist attempts to tear them from the tribe. This difference lies in the nature of the purpose on which they're founded. Cults are about the leader's greatness. They cultivate specialness in his image. Tribes are about mutual benefit in service of survival. As shared purposes go, survival is a good one, perhaps the strongest in a world where death is an ever-present threat. Hence its power to bind in a common purpose.

We see this same effect at work on a broader scale when survival of a nation is at stake. The French Resistance in World War II brought together different people from all classes of society in the common purpose of fighting the Nazi occupation. After the 2001 terrorist attack on the World Trade Centers in New York, the people of the United States came together in a way they had not experienced since the end of World War II. No matter whether they lived in Montana or Mississippi, Hawaii or Maine, they bonded with New Yorkers in their terrible plight. Indeed people from around the entire globe joined together in this shared identification. I will have more to say about this later in the chapter.

To sum up, I'm suggesting that the tribe is a better example of group consciousness than the cult because its individual members are valued and honored not for themselves but for their contributions to the greater whole. Their shared purpose is survival—not of any one individual, but of the entire collective. Cults too embody a group consciousness, but one that's defined by and subject to the whims of its leader. His ego has hijacked the group and yoked its individual members into subservience in order to satisfy his craving for adulation. Therefore the cult fails as a model of true group consciousness.

The Experience of Group Consciousness

The vast majority of us will never belong to a cult or a tribe. We live in neighborhoods, usually with very little connection to our surrounding communities. Where in our lives, then, can we embrace group consciousness and shared purpose? Examples are not hard to come by. Just look for places where you join with others in a common purpose that, for a time, supersedes your own individual goals and ego-based identity.

Sunset on the banks of the Columbia River, in a small park some fifteen miles outside Portland, Oregon. The director shouts, "Action!" and a young woman begins to jog in my direction. Children play loudly on a nearby swing set. Not far away, another young woman sits on the grass, her back to a tree. Charcoal sketches of the children at play are strewn about her as she clutches her arms to her chest, eyes wide in shock and confusion.

I stand on the sidelines as the camera tracks with the path of the jogger. She spies the artist, slows, approaches her, asking gently, "Hey, are you OK?" The artist begins to sob uncontrollably. She unfolds her arms, holds them out for the jogger to see. They are scored with a series of long, bloody gashes. And the director shouts, "Cut!"

I have honest-to-God goosebumps. Tears well up in my eyes. This is one of the finest, proudest moments of my life. I am present to watch as the characters and situations, given birth in my mind, come to life on this, the first day of the film shoot. So many people—actors, camera crew, the director, the guys who constructed the swing set and will shortly be tearing it down in the fading light of dusk—all coming together in the shared purpose of producing my screenplay, translating my words from paper into actual scenes and images that will become a movie.

*   *   *

A movie set is one of the best examples of shared purpose that I've encountered. The closeness that comes from working together in the making of a movie is unparalleled (except perhaps where survival is at stake). Each crew member is valued for her contribution; each one's contribution is recognized as unique and necessary. If an actor stumbles on a line, if the set is not lit properly, if the makeup shows, if the camera angle is off, if there is not enough food to satisfy the crew, if, if, if—then the entire scene, and possibly the whole movie, will fail.

Few of us will have the chance to participate in filming a movie, but many have helped put on a school play. I've watched my daughter running lines with her cast mates, coming together in service of a production that will be performed a mere three or four nights on stage and then be seen no more. Nonetheless, bonds were formed that lasted years. Working as a team in a corporate setting, surgical suite, or law firm can be just as rewarding in terms of closeness—provided that the team members value each other's contributions and keep their egos out of the way.

The intimacy of shared purpose can be so overpowering that it pulls us into romantic entanglements or sexual affairs. This occurs when people mistake the excitement of shared purpose for the intimacy of love, and it helps explain why Hollywood stars have such high divorce rates. Working closely with a costar on an isolated movie set over the course of a sixty-day shoot forges an intensely intimate bond that few spouses can hope to share in. The same holds true for workplace affairs. Simply attending a weeklong conference, especially if it involves workshops with personal sharing, can result in that same sense of intimacy and group identity—with the same risk of excitement slipping into sexual indiscretion.

But no matter how intense the event or how close the bonds formed, eventually it is over: the final scene is in the can, the project completed and delivered. The high wears off. People return home to their spouses and families. Or the project continues, but the team changes. People leave for better jobs, or get reassigned to new projects. That powerful sense of community, of group mind and shared purpose, fades into memory. It cannot last because it is not rooted in anything permanent or ultimate. The ego's dream world can get pretty heady, but one way or another, the good times always end.

*   *   *

The joy of my movie shoot began to crumble within days, when the lead actor arrived on set, intent on commandeering the shoot, shaping it to his liking, changing lines as he saw fit without regard to the story or its veracity. Because of his greater experience, he felt that he, and not anyone else, knew the right way to make this movie. The director deferred to him. The final cut was so flawed it was unsalvageable.

No matter how connected the group, the moment any of its members allow their own egos to rise up and dominate— the moment anyone insists, *I alone know best*—the group is doomed. The members either go along and allow this hijacking to occur—in which case the group becomes cult-like—or they rebel and the group rapidly falls apart under the weight of accumulated grievances. Without that shared sense of purpose, the joy and excitement vanish.

It took me months to accept the fact that my film would never see the light of a projector. But when I finally gave up trying to fix what couldn't be fixed and let my hopes go (in a moment as low and despairing as that first day on the Columbia River was high and inspiring), I was free to move on. The eventual result was my first book.

But just for the sake of argument, let's imagine that the shoot had gone well—amazingly well—resulting in an outstanding film. What would have come next? Applying to film festivals, getting bought by a distributor, trusting that distributor to piece together a good trailer, praying that the movie got good reviews, and on and on. With the best possible luck, I would have made some money or won an award. But eventually all that would have faded. Every time you watch the Academy Awards and those winners stand beaming before the crowd and cameras, brandishing their golden Oscars in triumph, know that they will awaken the next morning wondering, "What's next?"

How often have we achieved some goal and then, after the excitement wears off, fallen into a certain familiar emptiness, a longing for the next new challenge! It's an addictive pattern, really. The high has worn off. To counter withdrawal, we try to replace it with a new high, something even grander. *A Course in Miracles* tells us that the ego's credo is *"Seek and do* not *find."*[7] The ego wants to keep us searching. And so we join a new group, write another screenplay, take up a new sport, or a new lover, look for a better yoga teacher. But as long as we believe that our sense of meaning and purpose comes from outside ourselves, then we confine our search to the dim halo of the ego's streetlight. Neither meaning nor happiness can found there. You can't reach these by taking direction from Never-Mind. And so the fruitless search continues.

Breaking Down and Building Up: Entropy versus Life

There is very little that medieval scholars and modern physicists agree upon, as you might expect. But there is one doctrine that both have endorsed: all things in this world of time and space must come to an end.

Medieval scholars referred to this as the inevitable triumph of *chaos*: the empty, lightless, yawning void to which all life inevitably succumbs. In physics, it is known as the principle of *entropy*. Any physical system will always seek its most stable, lowest-energy state. Higher levels of organization inevitably give way to lower ones in a movement towards ever greater degrees of randomness, with chaos being the nadir. This holds true whether we're talking about your car engine, the pyramids, a hurricane, or your physical body. They will give out, disperse, collapse, crumble into dust. In the process, energy is freed up. This energetic release can occur as slowly as with the decay of a fallen tree trunk or as suddenly as an explosion. Either way, structure breaks down. Entropy and chaos win out.

The reason for this is simple. For any physical system, achieving higher levels of organization requires the input of energy. The bonds that hold atoms together as molecules are energetic bonds. The proteins that make up your cells and the nucleotides that string together to form your DNA don't just drift into position by chance. They require energy to come into alignment. But physics tells us that energy is finite. All there ever was, is, or will be is already present within the universe. Energy can neither be created nor destroyed; it can only change form.

Stretch a rubber band and you've invested energy that's now stored in the realignment of its chemical fibers. Release the rubber band, and that energy releases with a snap. But keep the rubber band extended for a year or more and what happens? Those fibers release their stored energy slowly as they fray and the rubber band relaxes back towards its original state. Eventually your rubber band will be useless. And how did that energy get imparted to the rubber band in the first place? You put it there when you stretched it. And where did you get the energy to perform that maneuver? From the food you ate, broken down and transmuted into muscular action by your body's enzymes. But how did that food get its energy? If meat, by ingesting other organisms or plants. If vegetable, from the sun. Ultimately, almost all energy on planet earth comes from sunlight. (The heat from undersea volcanic vents is a rare exception.) But even the sun is destined to burn itself out in a few billion years. We know this because we've observed it in other suns, other stars. Once again, entropy prevails.

Entropy and death are two words for describing the same process, only on different scales. If we think of life as a higher order of organization requiring the ongoing investment of energy, then according to the principle of entropy, that energy must eventually dissipate. Bodies wear down with aging (as do stars and galaxies). At some point, life becomes unsustainable and poof! The organism dies. The energy invested in its tissues decays and returns to nature. Entropy decrees the inevitability of your own personal, physical death. No matter how good your deeds or magnificent your achievements, whether saint or sinner, miser or spendthrift, wise woman or fool, your life here on planet earth will in time come to an end.

As we've just seen, however, entropy is not the entire story, or I wouldn't be able to write this and you wouldn't be reading it. The very fact that we are alive is an example of entropy's failure (however temporary). Life itself could be considered a project to counter the effects of entropy. And it achieves this through a process of coming together at multiple levels. Smaller, less complex life forms evolve and join with other life forms, resulting in more complex varieties of life. For example, every cell in your body contains mitochondria. These tiny organelles are the power plants of the cell, providing it with energy essential to its functioning. Yet each mitochondrion is itself a more primitive type of cell that was incorporated eons ago for this purpose. It contributes to the cell's survival and, as part of the cell, it is in turn provided with the nutrients it needs to survive and function. It gives and it receives in an ongoing, symbiotic, win-win relationship.

Life is collaborative—a joining together. Molecules are aggregated into proteins, fats, and nucleotides, which in turn comprise the components of every living cell. Cells reproduce and form tissues and organs; organs are coordinated in organ systems like the circulatory, endocrine, or immune systems, which interact seamlessly to give rise to healthy, functioning organisms—like you and me—that can then go about living, chatting, loving, hating, working, playing, building, destroying, eating, sleeping . . . you get the picture.

Life itself provides a powerful example of collaborative group consciousness in action: an affiliation of component parts that work together out of shared purpose to create a greater unity—a wholeness that is far more than the sum of its parts, but which seldom recognizes itself as such. At each level, the parts contribute by performing their specific function, and in turn they receive whatever they need to do so. When you chomp down on your cheeseburger or munch that kale salad, you're probably not thinking about providing nutrients to your cells or organs. You're just hungry. That's how the marvelous collaborative dance that is life operates. Each part knows its part and carries it out, but the whole has little or no awareness of those parts, nor does it need to in order to play out *its* part within the larger context of a higher order of wholeness. Knowing would only get in the way.

Imagine having to consciously monitor and regulate your heart rate or your breath. There is a rare medical condition known as Ondine's curse (named for a sea nymph from Greek mythology) that's caused by a stroke affecting the lower brain stem, which regulates breathing. People afflicted with Ondine's curse are able to breathe normally, but only if and when they think about it. Should they forget, there is no automatic mechanism that kicks in to restart the breathing process. Without the aid of a respirator, they pass out and die. To be forced into consciously focusing on bodily functions that normally remain comfortably out of awareness is indeed a curse.

Apart from these sorts of exceptions, however, the process generally works. Life is everywhere. And although no individual organism—no separate part—will ever survive death, the greater whole that is life continually pushes back against the relentless tide of entropy.

Rebellion in Heaven

What happens when one of the parts within a whole decides it's somehow different from the rest—a special case—and chooses to abandon its function, like the lead actor who commandeered my film shoot? Or what if this part yearns to go off on its own, to find its own way apart from the wholeness within which it played its accustomed role? The notion of the intrepid explorer driven to leave home and family in search of a better life is the subject of countless books and movies, and for good reason: it is the foundational myth of the ego.

The ego always goes it alone. Having defined itself as alone and separate, it has no choice but to embrace its solitary fate and elevate it into some grand and glorious purpose. The rugged individualism of Jeremiah Johnson, the entrepreneur who strikes out on her own in pursuit of fame and fortune, the spiritual seeker determined to win enlightenment by sheer force of will—these are all reflections of the ego's dream of self-creation. Forget God, forget your neighbor, forget the greater wholeness of which you are inextricably a part. The key to ending your discontent lies with you and you alone.

The seventeenth-century English poet John Milton, in his classic *Paradise Lost,* epitomizes this philosophy in his portrayal of the fallen angel Satan. After his campaign to unseat God has failed and he finds himself cast out of heaven, Satan boldly proclaims, "Better to reign in Hell than serve in Heav'n."[8] And although the words are literally satanic in origin, if we are honest, we must admit that we can relate to them. Or rather, our egos can. The fallen angel, spurning God, battling against impossible odds, is a profound symbol of the ego and Never-Mind. It is too proud to admit its error and submit. It cannot understand that submission to truth is not defeat; it is a choice for sanity. In this sense, the ego is like an oppositional toddler who, having just discovered that he has no choice about breathing, decides that he will simply hold his breath forever. He is outraged that he must give in to the need for air. He refuses to submit! He'll show them!

If we shift our point of view and regard such proud rebellion from the perspective of the whole instead of the part, its folly becomes even more evident. Can the goose leave the flock or an ant abandon the colony and survive? And what fate awaits our flock of geese should the leader refuse to drop back and allow others to take its place, convinced that only it knows the proper route? What if it then proudly steers them off course in its false certainty? What

befalls the colony if an ant decides to quit its boring, repetitive job and convinces thousands of others to join it in
its quest for liberation? What if the worker bee insists on
overthrowing the queen and replacing her?

Or, closer to home, imagine the result if one particularly self-aware cell in your liver grew tired of performing
the same old job day after day and decided it was time for
a change. It deserved better. Maybe it could train to become a muscle cell instead, because muscles do the heavy
lifting. Or a heart cell, because it enjoys pulsing to the
beat. This cell proceeds to shed its identity as a liver cell,
extricating itself from its companions and leaving home
to become something else. It wanders off and explores
the body in search of something better. Well, that cell
has just transformed and gone malignant. It has become
a cancer.

The liver cell will never succeed in going it alone or becoming something different, of course. Nor will you. Fulfillment is about inclusion, not exception. You can't reach
it by yourself. The Course tells us, "*The lonely journey fails
because it has excluded [from the outset] what it would find.*"[9]
In the reality of Ever-Mind, there *is* no solo journey, no
quest to carry out on one's own, because there is no such
thing as *on your own*. You were not created a thing apart.
You are an aspect of Wholeness. The concept of individuality only exists within the ego's delusional thought system, where it supports the belief that we are separate from
God. To find happiness requires that you first recognize
you are *not* alone and can never be alone. Like the liver cell,
you were created as part of a greater whole. Therefore that

is where your happiness lies. It's implicit in your very nature. In this you have no choice, because you did not create yourself, much as the ego would prefer to have it otherwise.

Impermanence and Opposition

We all long for home—the place where we are welcomed and loved with no preconditions. Home is where we feel accepted for who we are; it's where we feel we belong. But what or where is our true home, and how do we find it? For the ant, bee, or liver cell, this is straightforward and easy. They know what they are; they know their purpose, therefore they know where they belong. Home is all around them. They would never think to intentionally separate themselves from their group and "go rogue." But for humans, the task is more complex. Do we continue to live with our parents all our lives because that was our first home? Do we join as many groups as possible, asking of each, *Are you my mother? Is this where I belong?* until at last we find that one special group that welcomes us without reservation and recreates the feeling of home? For many, this is the impetus behind starting a family—to create our own special group consisting of our chosen spouse and children, all of whom will love us forever, tolerate our moods and bad behavior, and never reject us.

We face a difficult problem. Any group that we join as a physical being, that is, any group of individuals within this world, will turn out to be unstable, including families. Members will come and go, and even the most devoted of members will eventually be forced out by their death.

Such instability is unavoidable because the world itself is constantly undergoing change.

The Course tells us that any happiness that does not last is not real happiness. *"Elusive happiness, or happiness in changing form that shifts with time and place, is an illusion that has no meaning."*[10] And illusions must give rise to fear.

> *You can be sure indeed that any seeming happiness that does not last is really fear. Joy does not turn to sorrow, for the eternal cannot change.*[11]

At some deep level we know that our happiness will not last. This engenders fear—fear of its loss. Even as we rejoice, the knowledge that it must end huddles in the back of our minds, tainting our joy with a bittersweet quality.

As I stood on the banks of the Columbia River, watching the opening scene of my screenplay come to life, the high I experienced already contained the seeds of its death. As we noted, even if the film had turned out perfectly, my joy could not last. It was dependent upon circumstances, and when those changed and ended, so too would my joy.

By contrast, the perfect moments I described in the last chapter stay with me always. They are not saddled to any particular set of conditions that shift and change. They do not fade with time. And although the details of the situations that triggered them may grow fuzzy in memory, the experiences themselves have become all the more real for me—and ever more accessible—as I learn through *A Course in Miracles* how to let Ever-Mind into my daily life.

The durability of the perfect moment makes sense. Perfect moments are not unique; they are the same, no matter how or where they happen to befall us. The circumstances surrounding them will of course differ, but those are of no consequence. They are merely window dressing—a frame built by perception around an experience of eternity. The frame doesn't matter; it's what's inside the frame that counts. And what we find there, like the mirror in *Through the Looking Glass*, is not a picture, not a mirror image of ego, but a portal—one that reunites us with the joy of Spirit and Ever-Mind. The purpose of a window is to let light come through and to let us see what's outside our walls; the window dressing is just that—irrelevant.

*   *   *

In addition to impermanence, there is another, equally serious problem inherent in all groups belonging to this world that makes them poor vehicles for reaching Ever-Mind. With a few noteworthy exceptions, groups consolidate their identities through opposition to other groups. *My basketball team is amazing, but that rival team threatens our hopes for a winning season. I love my company and its products, but our competitors could put us out of business.* Your community, high school, college, company, religion, or country—each represents a group to which you belong, perhaps proudly so, but which sees itself in competition with other groups. What benefits one neighborhood adversely affects another (e.g., a new freeway). Even in the nonprofit world, charities elbow each other aside in the competition for major donors. And even if groups do not compete outright, they draw contrasts between themselves and other similar groups. All Protestant denominations grew out of Martin Luther's rejection of the Catholic church; all worship the same God. But they will happily describe for you what it is about them that makes them different and distinct from other denominations. Even within the *Course in Miracles* community there are factions, with some endorsing a particular interpretation, teacher, or even their own preferred version of the Course itself, in contrast to others.

We looked earlier at the powerful allure of tribes and cults. The sense of collective identity they offer their members provides a welcome anodyne to the sting of loneliness in a society that overvalues the individual. Yet the cult exists by virtue of its opposition to the norms obeyed by society. And however harmonious life within the tribe could be, there was the ever-present threat of war with other tribes. Such wars were frequent. Casualties were high. And if your tribe did not win, the result was slaughter, rape, and the enslavement of everyone you knew and loved—in a word, devastation.

The fact that group identity relies so much on opposition and contrast should come as no surprise. The group is composed of individuals, each of whom functions as an ego. The group is created, so to speak, in the likeness of its members and not the other way around. Group identity does not banish ego; it merely bundles and hides it from us—for a while. The joining together of egos is not true joining, because the ego is the child of separation and understands only separation. Within the group, we may allow ourselves to safely join with others, but the ego's imperative to preserve a distinct identity will find a way to reassert itself. We wind up emphasizing what's different about us, not what's the same. Either the group splinters apart, its members jumping ship for other, "better" groups, or it tries to cohere by attacking a different group that it has painted as its enemy. Either way, we are back to playing the game of Never-Mind.

In Search of the All-Encompassing Group

Group members are united within a group through their service to a common cause or purpose. However, if that purpose reflects some aspect of the ego and its world (as is usually the case), then so too will the group, and at some time, in some way, it will fall prey to the forces of opposition and impermanence.

Groups form around many seemingly different kinds of goals. Some want to win (sports teams, armies); others, to change the world (social justice), to make a profit (corporations), to help others (charities), to seize and hoard power (political parties), to share common interests (hobbyists), to teach skills (schools). Each goal will appeal to someone at some point in time, but none will appeal to *everyone* and *forever*. None is universal. None is ultimate. They cannot be. Within its world, the ego permeates and contaminates everything with the stain of separateness: its hallmark, its "original sin." Groups are no exception.

But might there be some cause broad enough to unite us all? Something that reaches beyond the ego and its craving for specialness?

*   *   *

A particular subgenre of science-fiction film portrays the earth under attack from an alien civilization (e.g., *Independence Day*, *Ender's Game*, *Starship Troopers*, etc.). In another variant, humanity is endangered by some disaster with global impact, like a plague or an asteroid strike. The appeal of such stories is undeniable, and understandable. We desperately want to come together, to transcend race, religion, and nationality. And how else could this occur without a common enemy, an opponent to battle? Yet even if the whole world were united against such an enemy, our sense of separateness would not magically disappear. It would find a way to emerge and subvert that common aim. We would disagree about how best to battle this threat. Or, having triumphed, we would find ourselves without a common enemy and therefore unable to maintain our united sense of purpose. We would fall back into factionalism and dissent, breaking up into smaller groups with competing interests.

Because the individual self is an illusion rooted in separation, we must face the fact that there *is* no group on any scale that can bring us all together. What we seek—as individuals and as groups—is union that requires no opposition: a group that will never break apart, never expel us; a group to which we can belong always; a group that welcomes all and opposes none. And *that* you will not find in the ego's world.

If we seek outside ourselves for what only exists within, we are guaranteed not to find it. If we search the world of form for the formless, the world of contrast and opposition for union and peace, the world of bodies for what can never be contained in a body, then our search will fail. We will seek, but we will not find. *"Seek not outside yourself. For it will fail, and you will weep. . . ."*[12]

If we want to experience union without opposite and feel the welcoming embrace of all-encompassing oneness— the ultimate group—we must look beyond ego to Ever-Mind. But the price of union with oneness is the loss of our individual self and all its cherished goals. To this end, the Course tells us:

> *Anything in this world that you believe is good and valuable and worth striving for can hurt you, and will do so. Not because it has the power to hurt, but just because you have denied it is but an illusion, and made it real. . . . For no one can make one illusion real, and still escape the rest.*[13]

How is this possible? How can anyone give up all they value? Only by recognizing that it has no real value; that in fact, by valuing it, they have cut themselves off from any hope of finding real value. They have bartered the gifts of God for a few nuggets of fool's gold.

Of course, it is no easy thing to recognize this, much less accomplish it. And the goal of perfect union with Ever-Mind may be a bit of a stretch. We are in need of help. And we have it, in the form of *A Course in Miracles* and our personal Course tutor, the Holy Spirit. If we are willing simply to consider what the Course teaches and try it out to even the smallest extent, the results we get will convince us we are on the right path.

Union without Opposite

Any group aspiring to a goal that falls short of Ever-Mind will by default serve Never-Mind. It is impossible to serve two masters. But might there be some way to join with others in a group that is not ultimate, but that is nonetheless devoted to a purpose not of the ego—a purpose that is in this world, but not of it? Such a purpose might seem unrelated to the pursuit of Ever-Mind or the perfect moment. But if it helped to bring us closer to an awareness of Ever-Mind, then wouldn't that be positive? It would not be serving the ego and its agenda. It would move the bar in the direction of awakening. When we join with others in a group whose purpose is to free ourselves from some aspect of the Never-Mind, we have done just that.

Alcoholics Anonymous (and related groups that follow its Twelve-Step model) is a fine example of this. The pathway to sobriety may not appear to lead to Ever-Mind, but it is certain that without sobriety, there is no way to get there. Therefore recovery from any addictive dependency (alcohol, drugs, gambling, food, sex, wealth) is a necessary step.

What is it about the Twelve-Step process that allows it to serve Ever-Mind instead of the ego? A group of drinkers meeting in a church basement to exhort each other to lay off the booze is not going to achieve the same result. In such a group, the members remain individual egos. By contrast, the cornerstone of the Twelve-Step process is the acknowledgment that the individual, ego-based self is *incapable* of recovering on its own. It is powerless. But when it surrenders to something greater than itself, a Higher Power (by whatever name you choose call it), and comes together with others in the shared purpose of recovery, then that joining is no longer taking place at the level of ego. The group becomes, not a collection of disparate selves, but an appeal to, and a forum for, that which unites us all.

The emphasis on anonymity in Twelve-Step groups further reinforces this truth. There is a common misunderstanding that the purpose of anonymity is to protect the identities of group members and spare them from being exposed and stigmatized as alcoholics. This is not entirely correct. Anonymity bolsters the recognition among members that their individual identities out there in the world, whether pauper or tycoon, scholar or dropout, are irrelevant to the group and its purpose. All are alcoholics. There is nothing special or unique about any of them or their life stories. They are united by their desire to be free of addiction. Nothing else about them matters.

This freedom shows up first as sobriety: release from the dependency on alcohol. After all, that was the original goal, the impetus for joining A.A. But sobriety is only the beginning: a beachhead, if you will. Those who stick with the program will eventually discover a very different kind of freedom. By turning their will and their lives over to a Power greater than themselves, their investment in all things of this world has lessened. They step more lightly through the illusion. They remain peaceful in the midst of adversity. They recognize their grievances and the danger in feeding them, preferring instead to let them go. They help others gladly, not as one ego to another, not looking to get anything in return, but as fellow beings united in the joint cause of freedom. They have become the willing agents of Ever-Mind.

We will have more to say about A.A. in the last chapter, but for now it is enough to realize that the ultimate dependency for all of us is not a particular substance, activity, or person. These are merely the forms the problem assumes in physical reality. The real problem, always, is the ego and the fact that we've mistaken it for self. Pursue the ego's agenda of *seek and do not find,* and an endless addictive cycle of desire, loss, suffering, and fixating on a new desire is guaranteed. But just as the alcoholic surrenders to a Higher Power, if you surrender the ego's agenda to Ever-Mind, with even the slightest degree of willingness, you change the game. You no longer operate at the level of separation. You belong to oneness, and there is no surer invitation for miracles to enter.

A Foretaste of Heaven

To conclude this chapter, I would like to offer one final example of individuals joined in a shared group purpose in which each member is equal and valued for her contribution, and where the whole, although composed of parts, is so much more than the sum of those parts.

In a choir, each singer has a unique voice which makes a unique contribution. The sopranos don't envy the contraltos, or vice versa. Neither is special. Members may stay or leave as they choose without the group breaking apart. New members can join at will, provided they have the talent and make the commitment. The result? Together the group produces a sound that no individual voice or combination of instruments can hope to duplicate.

When singing in a choir, your voice does not stand out, but you don't lose anything by it; you gain. Because what you hear when you open your mouth and sing is now the entire choir—all voices as one—and you hear this as if it were your own voice, coming from you. For this group, the part has become the whole.

> *What could conflict, when all the parts have but one purpose and one aim? How could there be a single part that stands alone, or one of more or less importance than the rest?*[14]

> *One function shared by separate minds unites them in one purpose, for each one of them is equally essential to them all.*[15]

And although the song will end—as all things do in this world of time—no one regrets or fears this ending. It is not a loss: not death, but a completion. The song lives on in your mind and in the minds of choir mates and the audience. Anyone listening can call it up from memory at any time with no sense of disruption, no bittersweet nostalgia over anticipated endings. The song exists in an eternal present tense, impervious to time and change. And again, what you experience is not your own small voice, but the resonant harmony of the entire choir: all parts, all voices, seamlessly joined as one in glorious song.

No wonder that Beethoven, in the final movement of his penultimate Ninth Symphony, chose to transcend the orchestra and elevate the music to its absolute peak by introducing the human voice in the choral adaptation of Schiller's "Ode to Joy." Beethoven realized that to convey the magnificence of God's love to his listeners and transport them to a climactic apotheosis, only a choir would do! "*We cannot sing redemption's hymn alone.*"[16]

The Course also uses the metaphor of song to express the idea of Heaven and its unity. In the supplement to *A Course in Miracles* titled "The Song of Prayer," we receive the following description of *true prayer*. It is the medium of communication between God and His creation—His one Son—as it was, is, and forevermore shall be when the ego and illusion are no more. The song of prayer and Heaven is:

> *The single voice Creator and creation share; the song the Son sings to the Father, Who returns the thanks it offers Him unto the Son. Endless the harmony, and endless, too, the joyous concord of the Love They give forever to Each Other.*[17]

The Course invites you to remember that you have an essential part in this joyous song. Without your voice, it is incomplete.

Who would not want to join in such an eternal chorus of Love? That is our overarching purpose, our one unitary goal, as students of *A Course in Miracles* and as the separated Sons and Daughters of God.

PRACTICE

Part One

Look back over your life and try to recall those experiences in which you felt yourself part of a group. Examples might include playing on a sports team, or joining an online chat group, a school choir, an event planning committee, a team project at work, a tour group you traveled with, a family holiday dinner, a protest march, a cancer support group, a Twelve-Step group. Other, less obvious examples of joining arise from sharing a common experience, whether positive or negative. These might include surviving a hurricane or tornado, losing a loved one to combat, making it through final exams, or something as simple as strolling down the street on a sunny afternoon following weeks of rain and exchanging happy smiles with those you pass.

Try to come up with as many of these experiences as you can, but don't force it. Write them down if you have the time.

Now review each one. Ask yourself the following questions.

- Did you feel you belonged in the group?
- Were you welcomed by *every single person* in the group? And welcomed equally? Without hesitation or reservation?
- Did everyone else in this group feel welcomed?
- If you made a contribution of some kind, was it valued appropriately along with everyone else's?

- In this group, did you hold any judgments about others and their roles that made you feel unequal: either inferior or superior?
- What caused you to leave the group? Was it of your own free will, or were you rejected?
- Did the group break up over time? If so, did this come about naturally as a result of changing circumstances or achieving the goal? Or were there other reasons?
- And now, the most significant question of all: which of the groups you listed made you happy?
- Were there any in which your happiness was ongoing and consistent and not just limited to certain special moments?
- For which groups, if any, can you not only remember what it felt like to be happy, but can still call up that feeling today, experiencing it as fully as you did when it first arose?

You're likely to discover that most of your experiences with groups were less than satisfactory. If you felt acceptance and happiness, it was only for a limited time, like my movie shoot. Or your acceptance was not shared equally by all group members. Some liked you, others did not. But overall, it's a good bet that none of the groups you were affiliated with brought you lasting happiness. And the reason for this was the intrusion of ego in some way, shape, or form.

Try to observe how this played out. How did ego worm its way in to break up the group and turn collaboration into competition? Look for its telltale signs, its preferred methods. Note these without judgment. You're looking back as an observer. Shit happens. Ego happens. You can't do anything about it until you first learn to spot it and recognize it for what it is.

You will find, ironically, that the groups which resulted in the cleanest, most honest happiness—the kind you can easily call up from memory and enjoy as if it were today—are often the ones that arose spontaneously, the ones you were least invested in, like the shared smiles and nods between strangers on the first sunny day of spring. Not much ego there. Just a shared appreciation of *what is.*

Part Two

Close your eyes and envision the entire human race, the whole planet, engaged in the only common cause there is, the Atonement: the task of awakening from the illusion that they are separate selves, with diverse goals and agendas, and all the suffering that causes. Be sure to include everyone—your friends, but also those you dislike or even think of as evil, whether you know them personally or only heard about them in the news. Exclude no one. Invite them all to join you at the table of the Atonement.

Now try to "see" in each being the one thing they have in common. Behind the facade of bodies, behind their separate personal histories, behind their diverse personalities, look for and find the expansive, all-inclusive Ever-Mind that you share. Feel its perfect, limitless love for you, and for everyone. Feel it flow across all seeming boundaries of time, space, and perception. No past or future; no here or there; no separate bodies, roles, values, or life circumstances to distinguish you from anyone else. You are one with all life, united in the perfect equality of the Love that is God's.

> *We are all joined in the Atonement here, and nothing else can unite us in this world.*[18]

5

'Taters, Alters, and Gems: Mending the Fractured Self

In the Gospels, Jesus was asked a series of trick questions designed to prove that he was a fraud. Among them, he was asked which commandment was first among all the others. Which was the most important? No doubt his questioner expected him to pick one of the Ten Commandments handed down by Moses on Mount Sinai, and whichever one he chose, they could then argue that he was wrong. But Jesus surprised them with a different answer altogether. First, he said, you must love God—totally, without hesitation or reservation, and with all your being. He then added that you must also love your neighbor as yourself (Mark 12:28–31). The injunction is famous: often quoted, widely misunderstood, and usually dismissed as being humanly impossible to carry out. But it is worth taking a closer look at this powerful set of instructions for life.

The first thing to note is that Jesus was asked which single commandment is first and therefore most important. Yet he replies not with one, but two. Or so it would appear.

For most of us, loving God is so abstract a concept that, although we agree it's certainly a good thing and we'd like to comply, we don't quite know how to go about it. Because when it comes to God, we are confused. We are told that God is love, pure and simple. But we're also warned that God sits in judgment over our every word and deed, and therefore God is to be feared. We can quite naturally respond to a loving God with our own love, but loving what we fear is a stretch. If we're honest, we'll admit that we have no idea what God is like, so the idea of loving God with all our being seems almost nonsensical. Nor does it help to admonish us that we may not understand God, but we should have faith and love God anyway. So we do the best we can. We craft an image of God, however inaccurate and inconsistent, and try to love it.

But Jesus then adds this second commandment about loving our neighbors. The notion of loving God may be too abstract to grasp or put into practice, but loving our neighbor is specific and unambiguous. Unlike God, we know exactly who our neighbors are. They are the people around us. We encounter them daily. But Jesus is casting a wider net than that. Metaphorically, we are all "neighbors," because we share the same world. In this sense, Jesus is instructing us to love, not just the folks who live next door, but everyone: those we know personally and those we will never know or meet.

Why did Jesus feel the need to add this second commandment when only one was requested? Perhaps because there is no second commandment. Perhaps because the two are actually one and the same: two faces of the same teaching. Could it be that you cannot truly love God unless you also love your neighbors—your fellow humans, each and every one of them—because they, like you, are also God's creation? We can take this even further. What if loving your neighbor is in fact the only way to really love God? It is the practical, behavioral aspect of loving God within the world, and so it naturally pairs with the first commandment. Viewed in this way, Jesus's answer makes sense.

Jesus doesn't just instruct us to love our neighbor, however. He says: Love your neighbor *as yourself.* Most hear this as a measure of how much we should love others. We should love and value them as much as we do our own self. But as we saw in chapter 1, we're not terribly adept at identifying the nature of self. We don't really know who or what we are. Therefore, what exactly is it that we should love? Bodies? Personalities? Life histories?

And what about those who are unhappy with themselves? Or who despise themselves, perhaps to the point of trying to take their own lives? Would Jesus's answer give them license to hate others too? To take others' lives? Obviously that's not what was intended.

If we listen to Jesus's words with ears attuned to truth, when he says, "Love your neighbor as yourself," he is not describing how much to love your neighbor. He is not making a comparison, that you should love them as much as you love yourself. Love is not measurable; it is not a quantity, not something you can place on a scale to weigh and compare. Rather, what Jesus suggests is that you begin to see your neighbor *as yourself.* That is, you recognize in some way that you are both aspects of the same greater Self and therefore equally deserving of love. Jesus is in fact helping us to understand how we can succeed at this seemingly impossible task of loving our neighbors. We do so when we recognize them as identical to us in the only way that matters.

There is a flip side to this. When we look on others with love, we drop our judgments and grievances—those patterns of thinking that keep us separate and apart from them. We are naturally pulled to join with them in the union that is love. Love sees no differences, no limits, no exceptions. Love is all-inclusive; that is its nature. It draws us together. In fact, unless we learn to love our neighbors, we will fail to recognize their true nature. Only in love's clear light can we see that we are all reflections of one greater Self, shining in the self-same love that flows from God to all of us.

But how is this possible, you rightly ask? How can I walk down the street, drive down the freeway, stand in line at the supermarket, and look on everyone I see with love? That seems harder than loving God. What about those who do not share my values—those nasty creatures who troll me on Facebook and threaten to kill me because we disagree about whom to vote for? How can I love *them*? At least God loves me back. They sure don't.

To answer this, we must return to the central question of this book: what are you? Start out with a false concept of self, and love becomes impossible—at least the kind of love that Jesus preached. Bring your self-concept back into alignment with God and Ever-Mind, however, and love becomes the most natural response there is. To everyone. In fact, it becomes the only response possible.

When you want only love you will see nothing else.[1]

You will be made whole as you make whole. . . . To give a brother what he really wants is to offer it unto yourself, for your Father wills you to know your brother as yourself. Answer his call for love, and yours is answered.[2]

In the sections that follow, I will attempt to convey a very different understanding of self, that is, of what you are and what your real relationship is with everyone else, and how we are all one within Ever-Mind—the only joining together that can never be lost or broken. Such a self-concept is so radically at odds with everything you now believe about yourself and others, however, that it's best taught, not through logic or reasoning, but with metaphor. What follows then are three metaphors, three different models that portray how the one Self of Ever-Mind can appear to be divided and parceled out among billions of beings who outwardly appear so very dissimilar, yet remain fundamentally one.

The Potato Heads

In 1952, a new children's toy was launched with the name "Mr. Potato Head." He was the first toy to be advertised on network television.³ One year later, after a nonexistent courtship and a hastily arranged marriage, he was paired with his spouse, aptly named "Mrs. Potato Head."

For those unfamiliar with this toy, a set of plastic facial features is affixed to an actual potato to create a humanlike face and torso. These can include eyes, ears, nose, lips, arms, hats, glasses, shoes—you get the idea. The result? Many seemingly different potato-head personalities, each wearing a different expression and sporting its own clothing style, depending on which combination of features and apparel you choose. (In 1964, new regulations required that the prongs on the plastic features be less sharp. As a result, they no longer penetrated the potato well enough to adhere, and the all-plastic Mr. Potato Head made famous in the *Toy Story* movies was introduced to the world.)

How does this simple children's toy help us understand the individual ego in relation to Spirit and Ever-Mind? Well, imagine one thousand raw potatoes in various shapes and sizes. And let's say you have ten different varieties of plastic eyes, nose, lips, ears, and limbs to choose from. You could easily assemble a small town in which no two potatoes looked exactly alike. You could give each potato its own background story. You could group them together in families (those sharing the same eyes or nose, for example). You would have your favorites, as well as those you weren't so wild about. And you could make them die off, or add new potatoes, or change their faces by replacing them with new features. But no matter how you dress them up, beneath all the plastic appurtenances, Mr. and Mrs. Potato

Head remain potatoes. Nothing more, nothing less. Their outer form is not their true nature. It cannot obscure their inner reality—their essential "potato-ness"—and its sameness with that of all other potatoes.

Obviously, this metaphor has its limitations. Potatoes really are separate (and they don't all look exactly alike), whereas the Spirit that lives within our minds is whole and one. But to the extent that the metaphor emphasizes what is identical in us over what appears to be different, it is helpful.

Let's carry this concept significantly farther with a more complex and far more accurate metaphor.

A Model of Fractured Self

Jennie looks in the mirror and brushes back her long, silken blond hair. Her eyes are a penetrating blue. Men find her irresistible. Her neighbor Julia, on the other hand, is plain, with mousy brown hair, brown eyes, and a perpetual half-frown that won't go away even on her rare good days. She worries she is overweight. She catches occasional glimpses of Jennie throughout the week and is drawn to her easy charm, but also insanely jealous of her. Julia once managed to steal Jennie's hairbrush. When Jennie found out, she got so furious that Julia had to go into hiding for two weeks!

Julia often hears Baby's soft crying coming from behind the door that's always locked. It makes her sad. She thinks Jennie hears it too, but can't be sure because, well, that's just how Jennie rolls. What Julia doesn't know is that for

Jennie, the door is never locked, so Jennie feels constant guilt over Baby. She dreams of rescuing her and taking her away somewhere safe, but in reality she knows there's nothing she can do. When she dares to sneak a peek into Baby's room, Sal is always right there, rigid in his big chair. He glares at her, and if she doesn't back off instantly, he rises and fingers the knife on his belt. Jennie has never seen Sal leave that shadowy room.

Fran lives there too, in the next room over, but neither Jennie nor Julia have met her. Fran doubts they even know she exists. She's only five. It's her job to take care of Baby and keep her quiet. If she fails at this, Sal punishes her. Which happens a lot. Because the only thing Baby knows are tears. And pain. So much pain. Will it ever stop?

What do these five have in common? What links them together in such a dark drama? Do they inhabit the same tenement building? Are they members of some highly dysfunctional family? Part of a cult? Or are they simply stage characters in a bizarre, postmodern theater production?

Jennie, Julia, Sal, Baby, and Fran are alternate personalities inhabiting the mind of a thirty year-old woman named Jennifer, who suffers from a psychiatric condition called dissociative identity disorder (DID), more commonly known as multiple personality. Each of these alter personalities (or "alters") believes itself to be fully real. Each has its own preferences in food, music, and clothing. Each believes that it inhabits its own unique physical body, with distinct characteristics including hair and eye color, right- or left-handedness, height, weight, age, strength, and abilities—even though in truth they all share the same body. And each can act independently when in control of that body. It doesn't matter to Sal that the body is female; he *knows* that his body is male. Each personality also has its own set of memories, some of which are shared while others remain closely guarded secrets. Looking on from the outside, it's obvious that these alter personalities are not "real"; they're by-products of mental illness. But they themselves would strongly disagree. They believe they're as real as you or me, or anyone else.

DID is an extreme example of a psychological defense mechanism known as *dissociation,* in which different mental functions, or conflicting aspects of mind, can co-exist side by side without mutual interference. You might picture this as train tracks in a busy railroad yard. They crisscross in places, but each train runs along its own separate track.

Let's consider a simple, everyday example of dissociation that almost everyone can relate to. You're wrestling with a problem—nothing too serious, but still, it has you preoccupied. You need to run an errand, so you get in your car, set your iPhone to a favorite playlist, and speed off. As you drive, you continue to turn over the problem in your mind, while also singing out loud to a song you know and somehow managing to pay attention to the road as well. You have three different mental operations running simultaneously in parallel. In a sense, there are three different selves, each involved in its own separate activity: navigating through traffic, listening and singing to a song, and grappling with a problem. Which one is the "real" you? If asked, you'd probably pick your inner voice, the one trying to sort out the problem. But if a cop car with lights flashing pulled up rapidly behind you, or if someone swerved suddenly into your lane, you'd instantly stop singing and thinking about your problem and snap into your driver self as your primary identification. You transition smoothly between these different aspects of self, depending on what the situation calls for. They are not in conflict, and you have no preference for one over the other. All three are comfortably ensconced within a greater totality that you think of as you.

Hypnosis offers another example of dissociation in action. In a hypnotic trance—essentially a dissociated state of awareness—you can be subjected to pain yet not consciously feel it. The trance state allows you to partition the pain from your conscious awareness: to dissociate it. Before the advent of anesthesia, hypnosis was frequently used for major surgical procedures. (In the final weeks of World War II, when the German army was in retreat and medical supplies were running low, almost all battlefield surgery was performed under hypnosis.) But how can we have pain and not feel it? How is this possible?

Through dissociation, the sensation of pain is split off from the main channel of the mind—the primary self—which continues to function as if pain-free. A star quarterback playing out the final minutes of the championship game despite broken ribs is using dissociation to block his pain with no need for hypnosis. He is so intensely focused on the game that the pain signals from his nervous system simply don't penetrate into consciousness. The game occupies the main track. There is no room for anything else to get through. So the pain is shunted aside. Similarly, with hypnosis, the pain is dissociated onto a parallel track of consciousness, like a train diverted onto another track to prevent a collision.

We can think of the hypnotized subject as using dissociation like a scalpel to peel away the part of her that feels pain, sectioning it off from awareness, storing it in a different compartment of her mind. But it's the nature of consciousness to always see itself as complete—to fill all the space it's given, so to speak. Therefore the part with the pain becomes its own entity, and the two resulting parts can now behave as if they were separate, conscious beings.

The subject's pain-free trance-self has become primary. She identifies with it; it speaks for her. It's on the main track. And it feels no pain, because pain sensations have been dissociated onto a separate track. But given the opportunity to express itself, that other split-off self—the one that still does experience pain—can come forward too. This gives rise to a very strange phenomenon: an experimental subject sitting and smiling calmly in trance, one hand bound with a tourniquet and immersed in ice water to induce terrible pain, while her other hand scribbles profanities to the experimenter, screaming at him on paper to stop because it hurts so much. That's how dissociation works. And DID is its most extreme manifestation.

Dissociation is a distorted process of thinking whereby two systems of belief which cannot coexist are both maintained. If they are brought together, their joint acceptance becomes

impossible. But if one is kept in darkness from the other,
their separation seems to keep them both alive and equal in
their reality.[4]

What causes DID? What kind of force is necessary to fracture the sense of self? Only extreme psychological trauma so severe and impossible to process that the mind has no other way to manage it than to split it off. This almost always involves horrific, repetitive, physical and sexual abuse committed by multiple perpetrators before the age of five. (Once past this age, the self-concept has hardened sufficiently to make such dissociative splitting much less likely.)

A young child has few resources available to cope with massive abuse. On her own, she cannot even make sense of normal happenings. She must rely on a trusted parent or authority figure to help her understand. Therefore she has no way to process the profound betrayal of a trusted adult doing things to hurt, scare, and shame her at night, for example, and then denying them utterly the next day, going so far as to accuse her of lying.

Of all the insults and injuries humans are capable of, betrayal may be the most difficult to move past. In my psychotherapy practice, I've worked with cuckolded spouses and smart, competent businessmen who needed a year or more to recover from betrayal by a life partner or trusted employee. How much harder, then, for a child! She can't run away or fight back; she lacks the cognitive capacity to rationalize, "My uncle is a creepy pedophile," or "My mother must be psychotic." Instead her young mind protects itself in the only way it knows how. It dissociates the trauma. It splits it off and sequesters it on another track. The humiliating, terrifying abuse isn't happening to *her* anymore, but to someone else, someone with a different name and identity: an alter personality. By implementing this defense, the child can safely disavow any knowledge of the abuse. She can lock it away and forget all about it as if it never happened, because to her, it didn't. But to those other split-off selves—the alters, the ones left holding the memories—the pain remains all too real. As a consequence, their agenda can be very different from hers.

Some alter personalities are desperate to tell their stories. They hope to free themselves from the burden of abuse and the suffering they've endured by bringing it to a caring human being. Others are not so keen about disclosure. For example, to an abused child, her abuser is the exemplar of what power looks like. Therefore, it is not uncommon for one or more alter-personalities to model themselves on the perpetrator. And like that actual person, they do not want their secrets revealed. They will threaten and punish those alters who tattle on them. *If you tell another soul, I'll kill you. And whoever you tell, I'll kill them too.* This is the warning that so many DID patients heard as children. Suicide rates are high with this condition, but not all are due to depression. Some are actually murders in disguise—attacks by abuser alters on those child alters who threatened to "tell"—to share their stories with a therapist. They truly believe that they can silence another alter by killing it off without harming themselves. They do not understand, or refuse to accept the fact that they all share the same body.

Each alter personality has its own motivating purpose: the psychological need that spurred its creation. Each holds a particular slice of truth related to that need. One might remember Grandpa as a playful and generous Santalike figure; another knows him as a nocturnal predator; while yet another believes itself to be Grandpa and continues to carry out his nightly reign of terror with the child alters in the imaginary space of the mind. With DID, the past is replayed endlessly. It does not fade into normal memory. It lives on, preserved perfectly by dissociation, as if it were still happening. Because to the alters, it is.

To insulate the psyche and protect its ability to function, the memories of abuse must remain fragmented, parceled out amongst the different alters. This spares the primary personality from having to remember them. As with a jigsaw puzzle, as long as the pieces remain unassembled and disconnected, no one will ever see the whole picture and have to face the horrific truth. And that appears to be a good thing, because who could function under such an impossible burden?

However, the fact that the memories remain dissociated and out of awareness does nothing to lessen their power. Just the opposite. Those with DID live in constant fear of truth breaking through, whether in a random memory, an encounter with a person or situation so similar to the past that it triggers a massive flashback, or an alter emerging when it shouldn't (like a miscued actor stumbling onto the stage) and speaking the truth that must never be spoken. This fear persists long after the actual abuse has ceased.

> *Dissociation is nothing more than a decision to forget. What has been forgotten then appears to be fearful, but only because the dissociation is an attack on truth. You are fearful because you have forgotten. . . . When what you have dissociated is accepted, it ceases to be fearful.*[5]

The real price of dissociation, then, is that the truth of the abuse can never be confronted squarely and accepted. Like shrapnel lodged deeply inside a wound, it interferes with any chance of proper healing. Because the memories stay fragmented and segregated from awareness, the painful past remains alive, unalterable by external events, impervious to new learning. And it plays out over and over in a perpetual, interior now.

Alters as Models of Self

DID provides us with a valuable model for understanding the nature of our own ego-based concept of self because, according to *A Course in Miracles*, we are not so very different from those alter personalities. We too are fragments split off from a greater totality, that of Ever-Mind, our one true Self. And like the alters, we stubbornly cling to our uniqueness despite the fact that it has no basis in reality: God's reality.

The alters of DID trust no one fully; they believe they are alone and must survive on their own. So do we. Alters form alliances with other alters for protection and to advance their agendas. So do we. Alters resist remembering the massive trauma that originally caused the mind to split.

So do we. Alters cherish their unique qualities and abilities, which set them off from other alters. So do we. Alters are terrified of uniting with other alters in a greater wholeness, believing it would entail the death of their own unique sense of self. So are we.

The only obvious difference between us and the alters of DID is that we actually do have distinct physical bodies. Or so we like to believe. But here too the Course says otherwise. The body, like the ego, is nothing—just another aspect of the world of perception. The body is the symbol of ego—its playing piece on the game board of illusion—while the ego itself is but a dark reflection of the separation from God, which never occurred in the first place, except in the deluded dreaming of the Never-Mind. So how different are we really from any alter personality in our conviction that the physical body is real, distinct, and separate?

> *Such is your version of yourself; a self divided into many warring parts, separate from God, and tenuously held together by its erratic and capricious maker [the ego].*[6]

Most of us have never experienced the sort of severe abuse that fractures the psyche and gives rise to DID. Such an extreme form of dissociation will therefore seem strange and alien. But the Course is very clear in saying that we are all using dissociation, all the time, to maintain a false picture not only of the self, but also of the world within which it situates itself—a world that does not exist. And this too has its parallel in DID.

In my treatment of this condition over the years, I have been struck by the vividness of the internal landscapes that the alters occupy. These alters see, hear, smell, and touch the rooms in which they live, places they've visited, and especially the scenes of their abuse, with a sense of reality that fully matches the way we perceive our external world. I have joined alters in musty sheds, empty churches, and graveyards. I have sat by their sides as they endured (once again) rapes and beatings in abandoned houses. I have playfully pushed a five year-old girl on a swing in a pastoral park, then later helped soothe her violent brother on a rugged, wave-tossed coast. These places don't just live in memory. They are not recalled fondly or with a shiver of dread. For the alters, they are reality itself, more real in fact than the external world.

*   *   *

We have said that DID is caused by severe abuse of a kind that few of us have encountered. What then could be the cause of our ongoing use of dissociation? What is the equivalent trauma that gave rise to our split minds?

We may not remember it—in fact, under the ego's dominion we do everything in our power *not* to remember it—but the separation from God was the ultimate trauma. Think about it. What could be worse than the loss of wholeness, our Identity, our true nature as love, and our connection to and completion in God? This separation shattered the One Mind of God's Creation into the myriad fragments of consciousness that we now identify as you and me. It gave birth to the ego and its world. And just as with DID, these dissociated fragments of Self now fear the resurgence of Truth. They (we) react as if God and Truth were a dangerous threat to be actively defended against.

> *Defenses are not unintentional, nor are they made without awareness. They are secret, magic wands you wave when truth appears to threaten what you would believe.*[7]

What are these defenses? Anything we utilize to maintain the belief that we are separate individuals. They would include specialness and desire. Also guilt, shame, judgment, attack, all forms of sickness and debility, and death itself. Illness and death in particular reinforce the conviction that we are nothing more than an impermanent physical body: a bit of dust and water that somehow tumbled into self-awareness. We think these defenses keep us safe, that our dissociation protects us from the greater threat of joining. But the only thing our defenses accomplish is to block the mind's natural ability to unify and heal itself.

How, then, can we mend the separation from God? In theory it's easy: we just need to change our mind, literally, and it's done! However, as long as we remain afraid of God and the oneness that is our true Self, it's not going to be so straightforward. Once again, we can look to DID as a model for our predicament. Because if dissociation is the problem, then its treatment should give us some clues about how our own healing can proceed.

The Path to Healing

When a patient with DID steps into my office, she usually does not know that she has other personalities. She seeks my help because of problems that have shown up repeatedly in her life, such as severe anxiety without any apparent cause; crippling headaches and other types of chronic pain; finding herself in strange places and awkward, frightening situations with no idea how she got there; blackouts that cover periods ranging from mere hours or days to entire years of her life; hearing not just one voice in her head, but many, constantly arguing with each other and urging her toward contradictory courses of action; and feeling so bad, worthless, and utterly disposable that she's seriously planning to take her life. In most instances, she will already have attempted suicide a number of times, although she's unlikely to share that with me when we first meet, even if I ask.

Eventually I come to recognize her problems as symptoms of DID. The headaches, anxiety, and internal voices are signs of conflict among the alter personalities. The amnesia comes from activity by different alters whose memories do not overlap with hers. Her suicidal impulses result from unremembered abuse and the toxic self-disgust and hatred it leaves in its wake.

When I inform my patient of her diagnosis, she rarely takes it well. Her terrible, shameful secret is finally exposed. The alters have been "outed." But I assure her, and any alters that might be listening in, that their condition is treatable—if they can commit to stick to therapy and promise not to hurt or kill each other in the process. I establish my office as a safe haven, a place where none of them will ever be judged (though limits will be set) and where everything that happened to them, no matter how horrible, scary, or shameful, can be brought to light—but only when they feel safe to share it with me.

I want to meet the alters, all of them, but they're reticent at first. They need to check me out, to make sure that my motives are pure and that I'm not just another abuser leading them on. They usually emerge one or two at a time, in clusters grouped around specific trauma memories they hold in common. Their abuse stories unfold in layers, like peeling an onion, with milder examples offered up first to test my reactions, or as a diversionary tactic, a way of preventing the more serious and upsetting abuse memories from surfacing.

I talk to any alter who comes forward, even if they threaten or curse at me. I never play favorites. They are all essential to the healing process and therefore equally valuable. I do want to hear their stories, but only when they're ready to tell them. I'm always looking for hints of other alters lurking silent in the shadows so that I can invite them to come forward. Some emerge with fanfare; others announce their presence through a single mysterious sentence scribbled in a different handwriting in a journal entry.

I've sat with alters who were paranoid killers, victimized infants too young to talk, predatory doctors, seductive teen temptresses, and TV celebrities. All were welcome in the safe space of my office. Eventually, all were willing to talk to me, because at the deepest level, they wanted healing.

They wanted wholeness, despite their fear of it. Many times in the course of treatment (which takes an average of seven years) I would think we were almost finished, only to have a new alter come forward with a fresh abuse memory that had been kept hidden, and which we then needed to work through over an additional year or more of treatment.

Initially, alters tend to be suspicious of therapy, and for good reason. They have not been treated well. But with time, patience, acceptance, and caring, they learn trust for the first time. As they reveal their tales of abuse and discover that they're neither punished nor shamed for them (by me or the other alters), they come to see that, despite their outer differences, despite the particulars of the abuses each endured, they bear the same basic pain. They're survivors. And they can join together for the first time, united in the common goal of healing from the past. In the process, their differences fade to insignificance. Persecutor alters who inflicted pain to enforce discipline now connect empathically to the child alter they once punished. The pain becomes shared, and once shared, it begins to heal. Old conflicts give way to a blossoming of love which brings them ever closer together.

The final goal of DID therapy is integration: helping the alters towards a willingness to let go of their separate identities, forged in fear and pain, in order to merge with the others. In the therapeutic crucible of my office, they have learned to see each other as friends, siblings, and more: aspects of a single group mind. The painful memories that kept them separate and apart, fearful of each other, have been exposed and shared with compassion. There is no further need to keep them compartmentalized through dissociation. And so the alters are free to merge. Like streams from different sources flowing together to become a mighty river, they can join as a single, unified personality, one that contains all of their different traits and abilities, yet is greater by far than the sum of its parts.

However, the final decision about whether or not to integrate is theirs to make. Not all alters will choose this. The pull of individual identity is strong, even within the same mind. Nonetheless, should they ultimately decide not to integrate, the trauma that gave birth to them, defined them, and kept them separate and in conflict, is no more. They are free to love and care for each other, to tackle life's challenges together with the benefit of their multiple creative perspectives, and to live a happy, full life as one more or less integrated self.

Healing Separation, Remembering Ever-Mind

If the Course is correct about the fragmented nature of mind and self, then our world can be viewed as one massive case of DID, with seven billion different alter personalities running around, trying to survive and thrive in concert and competition with each other. In which case, how on earth do we learn to recognize our sameness and come together as one? How are integration and healing possible with billions of "alters" who really do inhabit separate bodies?

If we take the treatment of DID as our model, then the only therapeutic goal with the breadth and power to unite the world's billions is the remembrance of our shared Identity in Ever-Mind. Only when we can access perfect moments—in compelling flashes at first, and then with increasing trust and consistency—will we accept that we're trapped together in the same ugly nightmare and choose to awaken.

The separation from God and Oneness is not confined to a few select individuals. It is not localized to any particular country, race, religion, or social class. It does not play favorites. We are all equally the captives of Never-Mind, all afflicted with the curse of ego, all paying fealty to its hollow idol of self. In a word, we are indeed alter personalities given birth by the separation from God. If we are to find healing, we must acknowledge this fact and bring forth in ourselves only what we have in common with everyone else, overlooking whatever seems to be different. And when we run up against grievances we find too difficult to simply overlook, we do not give up. We are willing to reconsider them, to rework our understanding of them, to release our flawed judgments, in light of what we are learning about ourselves.

A Course in Miracles calls this process *forgiveness*, and it is a cornerstone of the Holy Spirit's plan for awakening. (I will have a great deal more to say about forgiveness in later books in this series.) Forgiveness is the process by which we learn to let go of grievances: to overlook in ourselves and others the wrongs from the past that cloud our minds and prevent us from seeing the holiness in each other and loving our neighbor as our self. In this sense, forgiveness lies at the heart of the healing process.

Just as DID cannot be cured by the alters themselves, neither can our sense of separateness be repaired without help. We need a "therapist" who sees the truth equally in all of us and can steer us towards our own recognition of that truth. Such a therapist must come from outside the illusion of separation and bodies. He must stand firmly on the side of the truth, yet be capable of reaching us and working with us inside the delusion of separation, where we believe we exist. This therapist must custom-design the therapy process to perfectly fit the needs of each individual alter personality on the planet—all seven billion of us. Presidents and peasants are equally vital to the healing process; therefore he sees no differences between them. And this therapist must protect us from our own fears while refusing to spare us from the lessons we need in order to unlock the memory of our collective identity: that our "neighbors" are none other than our self, and therefore the only fitting response to them, in any circumstance, no matter how they behave, is love. Anything else perpetuates the illusion of separation and the need to maintain dissociation.

According to *A Course in Miracles*, the Holy Spirit is this Therapist. He reinterprets the world of perception with a single goal: to bring it into alignment with oneness and Truth. The Course refers to this process as *salvation* (or the Atonement).

> *Salvation must reverse the mad belief in separate thoughts and separate bodies, which lead separate lives and go their own ways.*[8]

*   *   *

If you bring to the Holy Spirit any problem or conflict, no matter how unsolvable it appears, He will show you how to look on it differently. The moment you do, the problem is gone. It solves itself, because no matter the form it seems to take, it is always at the deepest level a symptom of separation (just as the headaches, amnesia, and suicidality of DID were symptoms of the underlying dissociation). It may sound simplistic, but all problems have their roots in our false sense of self and the world that arises from it. With the benefit of the Holy Spirit's perspective, you begin to see they were nothing—an illusion—and with this realization they must disappear, in the same way that the most frightful of nighttime apparitions must vanish at the touch of the sun's rays. In the Holy Spirit's light, under His patient tutelage, dis-integration becomes integration and confusion leads to fusion.

But the Holy Spirit can't help you unless you choose to let Him. The best psychotherapist in the world can't help someone suffering from DID unless they first recognize that they have a problem they cannot solve, march themselves into the office, and commit to treatment. They must be willing to defer to the therapist's greater knowledge. They can't act as if they know better than the therapist. They can't pick and choose which instructions they'll follow and which they'll ignore. It's all or nothing. Ultimately, they either accept their therapist's vision of their wholeness or reject it in fear of what it means for them: integration into one whole self.

Now must you choose between yourself and an illusion of yourself. Not both, but one.[9]

*   *   *

We are always free to reject the help of Holy Spirit and continue to live as separate beings, split off from wholeness. That's the meaning of "free will." However, the Holy Spirit is an extremely patient Therapist. He will never grow frustrated with our lack of progress. He will never give up on us or reject us. The Course says He stands at the end of time. He's already seen the entire movie; He knows how it ends. He knows us as we truly are, or will be, at the conclusion of treatment, when there is nothing standing between us to divide us. So if we get fed up and abandon treatment at any point, He knows we'll return, eventually. Even if that takes lifetimes. He waits patiently until we choose to call on Him once again.

Integrated Mind

As we have seen, in working with DID, the final goal of treatment is integration of the alter personalities. In this process, the alters have willingly chosen to relinquish their separate identities and join together to achieve wholeness. They have no further interest in remaining apart, because what they feared—the trauma from the past replaying endlessly in their minds—turned out to be untrue. The past was finished, over and done with a long time ago, unable to hurt them anymore unless they allowed it to stay alive through dissociation.

As a result, their investment in remaining separate is diminished. The demarcations distinguishing one alter from another begin to blur and fade. Each may prize her unique contribution to the whole, but at the same time she increasingly comes to realize that to be made whole, she must be willing to let go of her separate identity in service of the greater, collective purpose of joining.

> *What could conflict, when all the parts have but one purpose and one aim? How could there be a single part that stands alone, or one of more or less importance than the rest?*[10]

What, then, does the end stage of "treatment" look like for the seven-billion-and-counting alter personalities who populate planet earth? As with DID, it has nothing to do with physical bodies, because bodies are part of the delusion of separateness. Bodies cannot join and become one. True integration takes place only at the level of the mind. Does this mean that we will pick up on the thoughts of others, or that (Heaven forbid!) they can read our minds? Not really, because those thoughts belong to the Never-Mind. They are unreal, a manifestation of the separated state, and therefore they cannot be shared. At the level of Ever-Mind, such thoughts simply do not exist. (That said, occasionally some bleed-through of thought does occur, especially with those we feel closest to. We label it "psychic," but it's just an inconsequential foretaste of one-mindedness.)

It will not be possible to describe to separated beings who remain invested in their individuality what integration might be like. We do get a sample, however, in the experience of the perfect moment. When consciousness expands beyond the body, how do other humans appear to us? Do they still remain separate entities when the unity of all things is revealed?

> *Each aspect of [God] is framed in holiness and perfect purity, in love celestial and so complete it wishes only that it may release all that it looks upon unto itself. Its radiance shines through each body that it looks upon, and brushes all its darkness into light merely by looking past it to the light.*[11]

In the clear light of the perfect moment, we may "see" the body with our physical eyes, but we do not credit it with reality. The body is just another false surface in the ego's fun-house world of perception. What is real is the light that emanates from the consciousness behind that body, a light that is shared. We see shining in them the same light, born of love, that lives in us. And that is all we see, because that is all that's real. Nothing else exists outside the vision of our oneness.

As I mentioned in chapter 3, *A Course in Miracles* refers to this state as the *real world*. We are now better equipped to understand that in order to reach the real world, it is not enough to simply alter perception. LSD won't get you there. It requires a realignment of self, the integration of you and your brother—you and your neighbor—within a greater Identity shared by all beings.

> *Accept as true only what your brother is, if you would know yourself. Perceive what he is not and you cannot*

know what you are, because you see him falsely. Remember always that your Identity is shared, and that Its sharing is Its reality.[12]

Father, You have one Son. And it is he that I would look upon today. He is Your one creation. Why should I perceive a thousand forms in what remains as one? Why should I give this one a thousand names, when only one suffices? . . . Let me not see him as a stranger to his Father, nor as stranger to myself. For he is part of me and I of him, and we are part of You Who are our Source, eternally united in Your Love; eternally the holy Son of God.[13]

Choose, then, his body or his holiness as what you want to see, and which you choose is yours to look upon.[14]

Here at last we have the answer to the searching questions we asked in chapter 1: "Are you my mother?" Are you my true self? Here too is the answer to the command of the Delphic Oracle, inscribed upon the temple of Apollo, to "know thyself." When we surrender the elements of our false self-concept to the Holy Spirit for His reinterpretation—our attachments to past experience (good and bad), to the body and its needs, to our cherished values and roles; but most of all, to our unique sense of specialness—when we do this, we learn that there was nothing there we needed, nothing worth holding on to. All were obstacles blocking us from a vision of wholeness and happiness far more precious than anything the world of separation could offer.

The Force That Binds

What is the force that reconnects our minds in this greater shared unity? It cannot be anything borrowed from the world of time and illusion. It must come from elsewhere, from our true nature, from within.

The Course tells us we are joined together in love, by love, because love is our true nature, the very essence of what we are. God is Love and nothing but love. God created us in that Selfsame image, so to speak. *"Love created me like itself."*[15] *"Love, which created me, is what I am."*[16] We will have more to say about love in later books in this series. But for now, this passage beautifully describes the relationship between love and wholeness.

> *As [love] is one itself, it looks on all as one. Its meaning lies in oneness. And it must elude the mind that thinks of it as partial or in part. There is no love but God's, and all of love is His. There is no other principle that rules where love is not. Love is a law without opposite. Its wholeness is the power holding everything as one.*[17]

Without love, there can be no forgiveness. And without forgiveness, which overlooks all the traumas and hurts brought about by separation, there can be no integration. Minds unwilling to forgive the past will not relinquish their specialness and make the decision to join. And yet this joining, this return to love, is nothing more than the remembrance of what always was and ever more will be.

Forgiveness takes away what stands between your brother and yourself. It is the wish that you be joined with him, and not apart.[18]

Everyone seeks for love as you do, but knows it not unless he joins with you in seeking it. If you undertake the search together, you bring with you a light so powerful that what you see is given meaning.[19]

When we join with our "neighbor" through love and see them through the lens of love as nothing less than Self, we heal the dissociative identity disorder that afflicts the world. When we love as God loves—without conditions, without regard to appearance, personality, or circumstance—the fractured selves of Never-Mind come together again as Ever-Mind: the extension of the Mind of God.

*   *   *

There is only one lesson that the Workbook for *A Course in Miracles* assigns more than once, and it states: "*I am as God created me.*"[20] If we could perfectly express this and only this, the Course tells us, we would instantly return to God and the embrace of oneness, and we would bring with us every other seemingly separated being. *I am as God created me* represents the final goal of the Course's curriculum. What we are has never changed, except in dreams, which mean nothing. We remain as God created us: forever One, forever Whole, eternally Love. All our searching was for naught, because the truth we sought after had never really left us.

*I was created as the thing I seek. I am the goal the world is
searching for. I am God's Son, His one eternal Love.*[21]

The Shattered Gem

I would like to offer one last metaphor, a parable really,
addressing the nature of the separated self. It requires no
further explanation.

Picture a radiant gem—a diamond perhaps—of the
most beautiful, flawless perfection. It is infinite, defying
notions of size. And it is alive with love. It is nothing
less than Beingness Itself. The light of awareness shines
brightly from within it, yet also radiates outward through
its countless facets in brilliant streams of luminosity—
great rays that go on forever and forever with no endpoint.

Now imagine that somehow the impossible happens.
This gem—this perfect, eternal diamond—falls into a
dream, a nightmare really, in which it is utterly shattered.
Pulverized. Nothing remains of it but the tiniest splinters,
billions upon billions of them, scattered about in profusion.

Yet because the original gem had consciousness, so too
do each of its broken remnants. Each miniscule particle
now sees itself as separate and distinct from all others. Each
believes it is unique, possessed of an individual "self" unlike that of any other fragment. And each part believes its
self to be complete, a whole unto itself. A dense cloud of
amnesia hangs over them, blocking remembrance of the
magnificent gem from which they all originated.

The pieces of the shattered gem soon begin to look on
each other with judgment. One splinter has an appealing

shape, another is hideous; one is much larger than average, another barely visible; one appears ragged and chipped, while another retains a glossy smoothness just shy of perfection. Yet no matter their form, and no matter their judgments about themselves or other fragments, deep within they all feel a profound sense of loss, a knowingness that they are somehow incomplete. Of course they hide this awareness from each other. Each believes that most other shards are content with their lot, so they pretend to be as well. Many are actually grateful that they're not even more shattered and miserable, like some poor fragments. But secretly, each knows there must be more to their being, a greater purpose which calls out to them.

As a result, each fragment undertakes a journey in search of its missing wholeness. They travel to other regions to encounter fragments that seem remarkably different. They undergo health regimens to make themselves stronger, shinier, more attractive. They listen to stories of oneness and participate in groups that promise to show them the one true way to reclaim their diamond nature. Most of all, they seek out relationships with other fragments. In particular, they search for that one special fragment, the one that will match their broken shape perfectly and render them whole—if only they can marry their jagged edges and bond them together in some permanent fashion.

But there's a problem. Because the fragments start their search for wholeness from the premise that they're separate and that their outer form reflects their true self, they've lost the capacity to understand wholeness. And so they seek for it where it cannot be found, among new and different forms of fragmentation.

There is another way, a better way. All that any shard needs to do is reawaken to its essence, its diamond nature, *and* recognize this same essence in all other fragments. Then the differences in their outer forms and their seeming separation from each other will not matter. Each is a precious gem, eternal and radiant with light. Their essence was not changed by the fracture. They remain purest diamond. And that has always been the case.

Can fragments such as these awaken to their true gem nature? Will they give up their fruitless search for completion within the world of splintered shapes and dissimilar appearances? Can they experience themselves as one with that original, flawless, radiant gem? And can they find the diamond light within themselves, and glimpse it as well in every other fragment, recognizing that all the myriad splinters and shards, no matter their appearance, are likewise nothing but diamond? Will they be willing to merge and join together in light—which is the only pathway by which they can bond and rejoin? Or will they cling to their uniqueness and refuse to give it up?

The vision of wholeness offers so much more than the individual fragments can ever hope to achieve on their own or in aggregate. A collection of shards and piled-up diamond dust does not a diamond make. Peace is impossible for those who see in pieces. But if they could give up their prideful independence from each other, their unique outer forms, their "individuality" as they see it, and most of all, their precious self-concepts, in order to reunite in the light of that original perfect jewel, then the pieces would return to peace and all would indeed be well.

Can the fragments do this? Will they return to oneness and peace? In truth, they never left. The shattering never happened, remember? The one Gem cannot be broken or changed. It was a dream. They need only to awaken. Will they do that?

You tell me. The choice is yours.

*   *   *

The Holy Spirit's function is to take the broken picture of the Son of God and put the pieces into place again. This holy picture, healed entirely, does He hold out to every separate piece that thinks it is a picture in itself. To each He offers His Identity, which the whole picture represents, instead of just a little, broken bit that he insisted was himself. . . . The forms the broken pieces seem to take mean nothing. For the whole is in each one. And every aspect of the Son of God is just the same as every other part.[22]

We are one because each part contains Your memory, and truth must shine in all of us as one.[23]

PRACTICE

The practice for this chapter is short, simple, and powerful. You can use it anytime and anywhere, beginning with this moment and continuing for the rest of your life.

Now that you understand your individual self as an alter personality, a fragment of something far greater and grander, simply do your best to look for that wholeness in everyone you see and meet. Wherever you happen to be and whoever you happen to be with—in the car, at the bar, at Thanksgiving dinner, in a conference, on a crowded city street, watching TV with the family—try to look past the bodies, the faces, and personalities to the light of oneness within.

If you find yourself focusing on these symptoms of separation instead, or if thoughts of comparison and judgment intrude, remind yourself that what your eyes are seeing is merely a surface impression covering over the oneness that lies beneath. Tell yourself that you prefer to see past surfaces. You prefer to recognize that these beings, these neighbors, are no different from you. That you are all alter personalities, split from the wholeness of Self, shards of the one shattered gem. And with this insight in mind, try again to look for what joins you. But not in terms of this world: not your likes or dislikes, your hobbies or where you live or work or went to school. Seek out that which joins you in Truth.

Perhaps you will find it in a sense of light that shimmers from behind the facade of a physical body. Perhaps it will come in an expression of love, a smile, a caress, an act of kindness—yours or someone else's. In whatever form it arrives, remember the love that binds us all in its gentle blessing. Love is all.

6

Wholeness in Action: "Miracles Are Natural"

When DID was first recognized and studied as a distinct psychiatric diagnosis, clinicians believed that most patients, once they resolved the traumas of their childhoods, would embrace total fusion as the final stage of treatment. Alter personalities would gladly relinquish their separate identities in order to merge and become one integrated self. However, this turns out not to be the case. The majority of patients whom I've treated prefer not to lose the alters they've come to know and love over the course of treatment. After all, those alters are reflections of self, and what's wrong with loving oneself?

Instead of merging, the alters prefer to remain separate and distinct, but without the need to function independently. They retain their unique perspectives, but use these to support rather than undermine each other.

Some take new names to signify just how much they have changed. Others keep the same names, born of painful abuse, as testimonials to what they have overcome. But their existence no longer depends upon any lingering, secret terrors from the past, cleaving them into pieces and dividing them from each other. Rather it is a choice they make consciously.

The alters have learned how to love themselves and each other. The love is what's important; the love is what binds them together, regardless of the different names they go by. Consequently, the symptoms of DID no longer plague them. There are no more confusing inner voices urging contradictory paths of action, no more embarrassing memory lapses or frightening intrusive flashbacks of abuse, no more suicidal despair or homicidal rage. Instead their lives proceed with an ease they once would have found unimaginable. Miraculous, in fact.

In this final chapter, we will consider the benefit to our own lives when we stop depending on our false, separate ego—to whatever extent we're able—and choose instead to realign with the oneness of Ever-Mind. We will discover that "*miracles are natural*,"[1] and actually far more reliable than the machinations of the ego.

What's in It for You?

Let's briefly review the evidence that brings us to this point. In chapter 1, we made the case that we are held hostage by a mental construct of self which I termed Never-Mind and which *A Course in Miracles* calls the *ego*. This false self-concept has no relationship to our true Self, the Ever-Mind, and no power over us except to perpetrate the charade that it is us.

In that first chapter, we arrived at the realization that no matter the problem or situation, there is only one real choice confronting us. We can fall back on the old familiar habits of Never-Mind or we can decide to be "in the world but not of it" and function as Ever-Mind. We used the analogy of a computer capable of running two diametrically opposed operating systems, OS1 and OS2. Depending on which you employ, you will get very different answers to your problems. OS1 promises peace—unconditionally, in all circumstances—even though the way in which that peace comes to you may look nothing like what you imagined. OS2 guarantees an endless futile search, designed to confuse and divert you from discovering your true nature, and doomed to end in death. And here's the catch: it is impossible to run both operating systems simultaneously. If you think you are managing that, trust me, you're running OS2. But only OS1 will solve your problems, because they are all *caused* by OS2.

> *Problems that have no meaning cannot be resolved within the framework they are set. Two selves in conflict could not be resolved, and good and evil have no meeting place. The self you made can never be your Self, nor can your Self be split in two, and still be what It is and must forever be. A mind and body cannot both exist. Make no attempt to reconcile the two, for [each] one denies the other can be real.*[2]

Remember, the Course cautions us that the ego's motto is: "*Seek and do* not *find*." Being incomplete, the ego must always seek for more; what other option does it have? But seeking, in the ego's case, does not bring answers, nor is it intended to. In this sense, the ego is like a busy restaurant that serves an endless variety of foods from all corners of the globe. You arrive there hungry, eager to try as many dishes as you can in the course of your one short dinner reservation. You consume them one after another until your belly is full. And although they seemed to have tasted good going down, not one of them truly nurtured or satisfied you. When you paid the bill, you were still hungry.

Chapter 2 explored how the Never-Mind uses perception to construct a world that appears to be objective and outside of you, a world so convincing that it crowds out all evidence of your true Self. But everything about this world is fabricated from the past, and the past no longer exists—if it ever did. If you buy into the world's reality, you also accept the ego and its judgments as real. You remain a willing prisoner to both. And although you do your best to cope, you can never escape from the weighty chains of the past or the frightening future you project out from it. The risk of sudden, unforeseen catastrophe lurks always in the back of your mind, along with the feeling that there's not much you can do about it.

Therefore, happiness, when it occurs, is fleeting. It cannot be trusted, because it does not last. And even when you find intervals of happiness in your life, the Never-Mind cannot accept them for long. Like a hyperactive child set loose in an arcade, it craves ever-new forms of distraction, bouncing from one to the next in hopes that someday one of them will last. Never-Mind cannot be at peace. Its very nature depends on conflict—although it will tell you otherwise.

In chapter 3, we sampled the perfect moment and the fulfillment that can be ours when the Ever-Mind steps forth to reveal itself—like a bright patch of blue opening suddenly amidst a sky choked with dark, threatening storm clouds. Such perfect moments are rare, yet as we saw, even the briefest exposure to Ever-Mind can change a person's life forever. They can also come and go without leaving any lasting impact beyond an appreciative, "That was nice. Now what's for dinner?" Either way, we cannot engineer perfect moments. Even with psychedelic drugs, it is possible to have a bad trip. Perfect moments come about spontaneously and unpredictably. If there is a guiding wisdom behind their appearances, it is beyond our ability to understand.

In chapter 4 we looked at the natural inclination to join together in groups. We asked the question: which is closer to the experience of the true Self, the group or the group member? And we highlighted the problems inherent in any group with a goal that falls short of absolute truth and Ever-Mind. Chapter 5 expanded our inquiry by considering three different models or metaphors that help explain how we can believe we're unique, separate individuals when *A Course in Miracles* tells us that in reality we're all part of the same wholeness: God.

All of which leads to the entirely reasonable question: why make the switch from OS2 to OS1? Why abandon the

Never-Mind, which, despite its failings, we know so well, and risk sacrificing our entire sense of self for this vague idea of an Ever-Mind that's so abstract, elusive and seemingly unreliable? What purpose is served by letting go of our alter-personality self and the world it knows in order to integrate with other alters in a greater oneness? We are not yet enlightened; we still function at the level of ego. And so, inevitably, we ask: what's in it for **me**?

The answer, of course, is abiding peace and happiness, and most would agree that those are worthwhile goals. But it's not so easy to picture yourself moving through your current life—going to work, picking up the kids, managing aging parents—completely at peace and radiant with joy—not unless you're in a TV ad for some new pharmaceutical product. Therefore, the more specific and practical answer to the question "what's in it for me?" is this: you will experience miracles. When you allow Ever-Mind into your life by choosing OS1 instead of OS2 at every opportunity, you will find that things just seem to work out for you.

It's not that your problems will magically vanish. Not at all. Rather, when you choose to see them from the perspective of the Holy Spirit, they all turn out to be the same, because they originate from the same source. They are by-products of a separate sense of self. Allow the Holy Spirit to mend that perception of separateness, and the problems resolve as well, in ways you never could have predicted, much less orchestrated for yourself.

However, before we look more deeply into the nature of miracles and how they come about, we first need to understand their opposite: the ego's operating system, OS2, and how it functions within its limited world of perception. After all, this is how the majority of us have conducted our lives up to this point. We need to be thoroughly convinced that it does not work before we will give it up and receive the miracles of Ever-Mind.

A Guide through the Mountains

You are a traveler in a distant land. In order to reach the holy city that is your destination, you must traverse a dangerous series of mountain peaks. At the base of the first mountain, a handsome and appealing young man approaches you and offers to be your guide. He claims to know the route well. He has traveled it often from the time he was a young boy, in the company of his father, who was also a guide, as was his grandfather before him. He talks with other guides regularly, so he's familiar with the latest weather patterns and snow conditions. How fortunate, you think, to have found such a splendid guide! You hire him on the spot and set out together, with him leading the way.

At first things go well. The path angles upward as you climb, but the view behind you is spectacular. You feel excitement about the journey ahead and anticipation of reaching your destination sooner than you'd anticipated. After all, you've chosen such a fine guide.

You enter the shadow of the first peak and the air grows chill. You come to a crossroads. The path splits, offering many possible directions to choose from. You look to your guide. He appears hesitant, but the moment he feels your gaze upon him he flashes you a big smile and starts boldly down the right-hand path. "This is the most direct route," he declares.

The path pitches steeply upward, twisting and turning as it climbs. It grows narrow, threading its way between a wall of sheer rock on one side and a steep plunge down hundreds of feet on the other. You step carefully. Your guide strides boldly ahead. You ask him to slow down, and he does. The path turns a sharp corner and—the way ahead is blocked by a huge pile of boulders. Your guide curses. "Obviously there must have been an avalanche in the past week and nobody bothered to report it." You wonder. The rocks are covered in lichens, suggesting that they've sat in the same place for a very long time. Nor do you spy any dust or scree in the surrounding area. But no matter. You and your guide have no choice but to turn and go back to the crossroads to find another path.

You retrace your steps and feel a sense of relief when the crossroads comes into view. Your guide surveys the possibilities and assures you that there is another route; it will just take a bit longer. You suggest making camp here rather than getting caught in the mountains as night falls. Also, by staying at the crossroads, you have a better chance of meeting other travelers. One of them may know of a good way across. Your guide smiles and shakes his head. If we start out right away, he promises, we should make it through the pass by dark. And he starts walking, this time choosing the left-most path.

The way is level. Easy hiking. The views of the distant peaks are breathtaking, but the path does not veer in their direction. It continues on, paralleling the mountains, gain-ing nothing in elevation. You ask your guide if this can be right. He assures you that soon you will come upon a broad valley that cuts right through the mountains. There you can easily make the crossing without danger. It's still a good ten kilometers ahead, however. Maybe more. Actually, he isn't sure, because he doesn't come this way often. He doesn't need to when the other path is clear.

You trudge on. Your enjoyment of the view diminishes and your anxiety ratchets up a notch as the sun sinks toward the horizon with no sign of any valley or pass where you might begin the crossing. Twilight descends, and you notice that the mountains now seem further away. And you have less elevation. The path is not climbing, it's descending! It's leading you *away* from your goal. You question your guide. He looks dejected. He's not sure why this is happening, but he does not apologize. Instead he suggests you continue onward.

You refuse. You need time to consider. You no longer trust this guide, but you can't navigate this unknown land by yourself. You admit to yourself that you are lost. But you have no one else to turn to, so you consent to walk a bit farther.

When it gets too dark to see the path ahead, you make camp. The following morning you rise with the sun and continue walking. Hours pass and still no sign of any valley. You tell the guide you want to return to town and rest. In reality, you want to hire a new guide. He says, "Fine, then you go back." He intends to keep walking until he finds that darned pass. You ask for your money back. Even a partial refund. He tells you you're crazy; if you decide to give up and retreat when you're already this far along, it's hardly his problem. Reluctantly, you begin the trek back to the crossroads alone, and from there back to where you started.

Of course, this is the happy-ending version of the story. In other versions, the guide leads you on and on until you both run out of food and starve. Or you never question his ability and waste several years wandering with him in grand circles. Or he abandons you somewhere high in the mountains. Or walks you right off the side of a cliff at night. In no version of the story do you make it across to your destination, because, the truth is, your guide does not know the way. He's as lost as you are, or worse, he's delusional, insane, believing he's a guide when in fact he's never before left the boundaries of his little village. When you tied your fate to this unreliable guide, you made a very poor choice.

The ego is just such a guide. However, unlike in the story, you never give up on the ego. You willingly let it lead you down one path after another, ever hopeful that this time you'll find the elusive pass through the mountains, this time you'll reach your desired destination. You believe that the outcome depends only on choosing the correct path, when your real choice involves, not the path, but the guide.

Other cautionary tales illustrate this same point. Folk-singer Pete Seeger's 1967 song "Waist Deep in the Big Muddy" tells the story of an army platoon on maneuvers in Louisiana. It's led by a captain determined to ford a dangerous river, the "Big Muddy" of the title. He's certain it's safe because only a mile upriver he himself had made the crossing. As the depth of the waters rises from knee to waist to neck level, and despite his sergeant's repeated, anxious warnings, this captain pushes on, until finally he slips in the strong current and drowns. The sergeant immediately reverses course and his men escape the same fate, but barely. As the song says, "We were lucky to escape from the Big Muddy / When the big fool said to push on."

What went wrong here? Unbeknownst to the captain, another stream had entered the river between the point where he'd safely crossed and where he tried to ford it with his platoon. As a result, the water was deeper and the current far stronger than he'd remembered. Yet still he recklessly pushed on.

Like the captain of this song, the ego is a proud and determined leader. Once launched on a particular course of action, it persists, oblivious to the mounting evidence that it's on the wrong track. Why does the captain ignore the deepening waters? What is the actual cause of his unnecessary death? Is it his pigheadedness? The arrogance of rank perhaps? Or a symptom of some deeper character flaw? If we view his behavior as a consequence of any of these, we will miss the real reason for his death. It's not his stubbornness that destroys him; it's his false sense of certainty. He has crossed this river before, recently we presume. His memory of the past conflicts with present experience. And which does he choose to believe? The past—that all-purpose determinant of ego-based action. If that past is accurate, he should be able to cross safely. In defiance of the mounting evidence that he might be wrong, he persists. That's his mistake, and it proves fatal.

Cause and Effect

The ego lives by the laws of cause and effect. An action taken in the past leads to another in the present, which in turn provokes a reaction of some kind in the future, which will lead to yet another action—like billiard balls colliding along neat linear trajectories. There are three noteworthy assumptions inherent in this understanding of cause and effect. First is the notion that actions (like billiard balls) are separate and distinct, having a clear starting point and a defined finish. Second, they take place in an external, objective reality independent of the mind of the observer. And third, that actions unfold in a linear time sequence in which the past drives the present, which in turn gives birth to the future. One action must precede the next. Without the first, the second does not occur. Therefore, the first *causes* the second. Cause always precedes effect.

The problem here is that for any given effect, we can assign multiple causes. If you have a car accident driving home from work, was it caused by the careless driver who drifted into your lane, by your inattention, by your angry mood that led to your inattentiveness, or by your boss who insisted you stay late to finish a report, thereby situating you on that particular stretch of road at the precise moment that a careless driver strayed across the midline? We could say, all of the above, for all are accurate.

Or we could delve still deeper. Why was the other driver so careless? What caused him to drift? An extra drink after work? Anxiety about arriving late for his daughter's softball game? Or maybe he was just absorbed in a song he liked.

But then we must ask (if we seek the "true" cause), who introduced him to that song? Who gave him his first taste of alcohol? Who got his daughter involved in softball? Might we logically infer that, if he had no daughter, there would have been no accident, and therefore it's all *her* fault?

As you can see, cause and effect is a slippery construct. It leads in circles—or, rather, spirals, each looping out in a larger arc, spinning off new possibilities, which in turn open onto infinitely more "causes" for whatever took place. The principle of cause and effect (which, like perception itself, seems so self-evident) turns out to rest on the shakiest of foundations. We never do know the "real" reason why anything happens. The limits inherent in perception guarantee this. As we saw in chapter 2, the ego is incapable of comprehending the entire picture.

There is an important parallel here with DID and its treatment. Alter personalities regard themselves as real, unique, and independent of one another. But the therapist must not join them in their false conviction if the treatment is to succeed. Even though the therapist interacts with each alter as if it were real, separate, and distinct, she must always keep in mind that they are aspects of a greater unity—imaginary parts within a very real whole. In the same way, we who see ourselves as private minds and separate bodies must be willing to defer to the Holy Spirit's vision of us and our implicit unity if we hope to override the ego's OS2 and experience miracles.

Since you believe that you are separate, Heaven presents itself to you as separate, too. Not that it is in truth, but that the link that has been given you to join the truth may reach to you through what you understand.[3]

Shifting Perception with the Holy Spirit

Miracles arise from OS1. They have no relation to cause and effect (not unless we understand that God is the only Cause and we are His effect). Miracles are not the product of saintly behavior, holy relics, visualization exercises, or intercession by angelic beings. According to the Course, miracles are the natural result of our realignment with oneness, that is, our willing suspension of Never-Mind in favor of Ever-Mind. When we decide to put OS2 on hold and flip the switch to OS1, perception shifts, quite literally, because we have placed ourselves under a different set of laws that do not obey cause and effect. We place ourselves under the laws of wholeness, not separation.

A miracle inverts perception which was upside down before, and thus it ends the strange distortions that were manifest. Now is perception open to the truth.[4]

Miracles violate every law of reality as this world judges it. Every law of time and space, of magnitude and mass is transcended, for what the Holy Spirit enables you to do is clearly beyond all of them.[5]

Because we remain convinced of our separateness, however, we cannot achieve this realignment by ourselves. We're too lost, too deluded. Like the alters of DID, we need help from outside—the help of a master Therapist. And that is the Holy Spirit.

Like the earthly therapist treating DID, the Holy Spirit is privileged with an overview that we are lacking. Because He operates outside of time, from the vantage of eternity, He already knows all possible permutations and outcomes. If we return to the example of hiring a guide to lead us safely through the mountains, the Holy Spirit would be no earthly guide. He would be akin to a flawless GPS system drawing data from a series of satellites monitoring in real time the global weather patterns and the local condition of all trails. Better still, its algorithms accurately predict all future conditions. It would lead you safely through the mountains, adjusting its guidance instantly to account for any pertinent changes. No human guide could hope to gain such a comprehensive overview, especially not one who is himself lost or deluded.

> *You know not where you go. But One Who knows goes with you. Let Him lead you.*[6]

> *The Holy Spirit is my only Guide. He walks with me in love. And I give thanks to Him for showing me the way to go.*[7]

Of course, our lives involve many more choices than those confronting a traveler on a narrow trail through the mountains. We are faced with hundreds of possible choices, thousands perhaps, in the span of a single day: what actions to take and not take, how to prioritize those actions, which specific words to speak, and so on. The majority of these decisions are trivial; we make them in an instant, almost without awareness, and they leave no lasting imprint on our lives. But they do affect our mood, coloring our emotional state and boosting or diminishing our capacity for happiness. Moreover, they also affect everyone around us as they pick up on our mood and radiate it out in turn to everyone in their vicinity. In this sense, even our seemingly trivial choices have the potential to influence thousands.

To better understand this, let's turn to another metaphor borrowed from the world of childhood: the game of pickup sticks. For those unfamiliar with the game, a bundle of sticks, uniform in length and thickness, are tossed down to make a random, jumbled pile. Players take turns attempting to pick up the sticks one at a time without disturbing any of the other sticks. If they remove a stick successfully, they count it theirs and gain another turn. If, however, they jostle or move any other stick, they lose their turn and the next player gets a try. When all sticks have been gathered, whoever has the most in their possession wins the game.

In order to win, two skills are necessary: a steady hand and the ability to discern which sticks are the least encumbered and therefore most ready to be plucked. This is not always obvious. If a player focuses too narrowly on one particular stick, she may miss entanglements that will wind up jostling other sticks. It is essential to view the positioning of each stick within the greater context of the entire pile.

It is not too difficult to imagine your life, or any given day in your life, as a jumbled pile of pickup sticks. Which tasks or errands do you identify as priorities, and why? Which may seem small, but nonetheless warrant your attention? And which are too remote or irrelevant to worry about for the time being? Making sure you have gas in the car or milk for the baby may seem like no big deal, but the consequences of inaction could be unpleasant. On the other hand, if your smoke detector has just sounded with a piercing screech that's got the dog howling and the kids in tears, then that will override all other considerations.

We play life's game of pickup sticks to the best of our ability, trying to see as much of the big picture as possible. But sticks do get bumped. Sometimes the entire pile gets tossed into upheaval. Given the limits of our vision, the unsteadiness of our decision-making process, and the clumsiness of its implementation, this is inevitable. We've learned to accept it.

What happens when we turn life's game of pickup sticks over to the Holy Spirit? He knows exactly the positioning of each stick and how it's balanced with respect to all others. He is aware of the subtlest intersection points, both at the surface level and buried within the deeper layers. He knows how a minor shift in one part of the pile can set off an avalanche elsewhere. We are not privy to such an overview. The result is that Holy Spirit can direct us toward which stick to pick up and how best to go about it. The jumbled, chaotic pile vanishes before our eyes as stick after stick comes away cleanly and effortlessly. Eventually, as the pile dwindles down to a few sticks, it becomes easy to spot the ones that are ripe for the picking. Our trust in the process grows as anxiety diminishes. We face the next round with a confidence that is not born of the ego.

This process of turning our complex, interlocking problems over to Holy Spirit will work every time. It does not depend on other people or circumstances, nor does it matter how you happen to view the problem—whether you judge it easy to solve or utterly impossible. That's the very essence of miracles. You can't see the path forward, you may be blinded to the potential consequences of your decisions, but the Holy Spirit is not.

There's one hitch, however. In order to benefit from such flawless guidance, you have to get out of the way. As we've said before, you must consciously make the switch from OS2 to OS1. If the guidance of the Holy Spirit instructs you to lift a particular stick, but you overrule it because, in this one instance, you're certain you know better—you spy a more obvious choice from a different part of the pile—then you lose access to His help. You've shut Him out. If you turn off your GPS because your boyishly exuberant guide insists that this time he really, truly does know the way, you will have no one to blame but yourself.

The Power of Surrender

How do we get out of the way? What does that look like? Fortunately, we have a time-tested model in the first three steps of Alcoholics Anonymous (A.A.) and other similar Twelve-Step programs.

Step One

"We admitted we were powerless over alcohol [substitute here any addictive attachment you have, or simply the ego itself]—that our lives had become unmanageable."

Step Two

"Came to believe that a Power greater than ourselves could restore us to sanity."

Step Three

"Made a decision to turn our will and our lives over to the care of God as we understood Him."[8]

Let's consider these steps one at a time to illustrate how the process works and its application to all aspects of our lives. It's important to understand, however, that every step is essential, and each rests on the previous step. Skipping ahead will not work; it will only delay us.

First, we must admit to ourselves that we are powerless over our lives, and that they have become unmanageable. For alcoholics, this step is rather straightforward, though by no means easy. By the time they're willing to consider A.A., they have hopefully "hit bottom"—that is, their drinking has wrought sufficient havoc on both their personal and work lives that it can no longer be denied. Further, they have tried multiple times to quit, or at least limit, their drinking—and failed. All that Step One asks is an honest reckoning.

For the nonalcoholic, this first step can be more difficult, because at first glance, life appears quite manageable. OK, not everything has proceeded smoothly. You've endured frustrations, major disappointments, even some failures. But every time you were knocked down, you dusted yourself off and climbed back into the ring. Therefore, when faced with this first step, your Never-Mind protests that it's simply not true; it doesn't apply to you. The ego regards it as insulting. How dare they ask you to admit that you are powerless, that your life is out of control? Like that dishonest mountain guide, the ego will always have some excuse at the ready to explain why things haven't gone as planned. It's usually someone else's fault or the result of circumstances out in the world and beyond your control. The ego will do all in its power to seduce you back into complacency and maintain its grip on your life.

For this reason, Step One can take years to play out. Only after we've ridden the ego's roller-coaster and had our fill of its highs and lows are we ready to admit that life under the rule of ego is indeed unmanageable, and that by putting it in charge and letting it run amok, we have abdicated our power. Unfortunately, for most of us a certain degree of suffering is necessary before we're ready to accept this, overrule the ego and embrace real change.

How could this readiness be reached save through the sight of all your misery, and the awareness that your plan has failed, and will forever fail to bring you peace and joy of any kind?[9]

Tolerance for pain may be high, but it is not without limit. Eventually everyone begins to realize, however dimly, that there must be a better way.[10]

To arrive at this realization, we must become alert to the ego's clever manipulations. We must cultivate an ongoing vigilance for its bait-and-switch tactics, its sleight-of-hand diversions. Because the ego will promise change, and it will deliver. However, that change will be superficial—not real change, but the exchange of one form of suffering for another, one illusion for a "better" one. Like a game of whack-a-mole, you snuff out the problem you see only to have it reappear elsewhere and in another form.

> *A problem can appear in many forms, and it will do so while the problem lasts. It serves no purpose to attempt to solve it in a special form. It will recur and then recur again and yet again, until it has been answered for all time and will not rise again in any form.*[11]

Remember, the ego's world is governed by cause and effect, where the true cause of the problem—the ego itself—can never be acknowledged, much less corrected. Therefore it can only act at the level of the effect. It cannot address true cause, for that would require it to eradicate itself, which it will never do. In medicine, this would be equivalent to treating the symptom, not the underlying disease. If your doctor prescribes opiates to reduce your abdominal pain when the cause of that pain is a ruptured appendix, you may briefly feel some relief, but the treatment could prove fatal.

In A.A., Step One addresses powerlessness only as it relates to alcohol. *A Course in Miracles* extends this insight much further. To make the shift to OS1 and Ever-Mind, we must be willing to turn *everything* over to the Holy Spirit. There can be no exceptions, no areas of our lives, however seemingly small, where we decide that we know best and remain in charge. That's why this first step is so challenging.

Whenever we encounter a problem, we reflexively boot up OS2 and retreat back into the arms of ego. Even though we know better, it's how we've always lived. It's too familiar.

From its earliest lessons, *A Course in Miracles* confronts us with our inability to understand the meaning of anything, much less what to do about it. Some examples of this—all coming within the first twenty-five lessons of the Workbook—include: "*I do not understand anything I see*"; "*I am never upset for the reason I think*"; "*My thoughts do not mean anything*"; "*I do not perceive my own best interests*"; and "*I do not know what anything is for.*"[12]

These salient passages leave no room for doubt about our ignorance:

> *I do not know what anything, including this, means. And so I do not know how to respond to it. And I will not use my own past learning as the light to guide me now.*[13]

> *I do not know the thing I am, and therefore do not know what I am doing, where I am, or how to look upon the world or on myself.*[14]

The takeaway could not be clearer. When we identify with ego and operate as if we were separate beings, we truly cannot understand anything. Once again, the ego interprets such statements as insulting—repudiations of our abilities and intelligence—but in fact they are just the opposite. Only by acknowledging that illusions have no power and divesting ourselves of them can we access true Power through the Ever-Mind and OS1.

*   *   *

Step Two in Alcoholics Anonymous is the natural follow-up to Step One. Having admitted that our lives were unmanageable and having recognized the powerlessness of the ego, we naturally ask: where, then, does power lie? It cannot be in anything of this world. We (or someone we know) has tried every remedy this world has to offer and found them all wanting. Instead we "came to believe that a Power greater than ourselves could restore us to sanity." Step Three carries this to its logical conclusion: that greater Power is God. What else could it be? However, *God* is such a buzzword, so maligned and misunderstood in our culture, that for many it's easier to conceptualize God as a Higher Power in whatever way fits most comfortably with their understanding. Any God about Whom we remain skeptical or have reservations would not be welcomed into our lives. Note, however: nowhere in Steps Two or Three does it say that we must *believe* in God. The steps are not about belief; they are not theoretical, but entirely practical. We come to believe that a Power greater than ourselves, whatever Its nature, has the ability to restore us to sanity, and that we do not.

Some might balk at the notion that they're somehow lacking sanity. The alcoholic's world is indeed insane, but not ours. Yet, as we saw in chapter 2, the world of perception, in which we all believe, can hardly be considered rational and sane. Alcoholics hold no monopoly on insanity. In fact, the Course defines *sin*—the thing we need to be saved from—not as wrongdoing, but wrong-mindedness, that is, insanity. We are not bad; we are merely mad.

Sin is insanity. It is the means by which the mind is driven mad, and seeks to let illusions take the place of truth. And being mad, it sees illusions where the truth should be, and where it really is.[15]

In which case, we have all been driven insane by the ego.

A.A. tells us that the cure for our madness lies in a Power greater than ourselves. The Course calls that Power the Holy Spirit, but you could just as easily refer to it as God, the Universe, the Tao, or George Lucas's "Force." The name doesn't matter, only the decision "to turn our will and our lives over to the care of God as we understood Him."

This turning-over process does not happen by itself. We do not passively acquiesce. It requires a conscious decision. As we've noted throughout this book, and as the Course reminds us over and over, our ability to choose is the only real power we have left in our delusional state of mind. Even amidst florid insanity, we retain this power of decision—the ability to choose which OS we want to run at any given time. Having made that choice, the rest follows inevitably. Absent this decision, nothing changes.

The Holy Spirit does not force-feed freedom to you, because that would violate free will. It would no longer be freedom. He waits patiently, until you are fully ready, until you call out to Him in recognition that your will—what you want for yourself—in no way differs from His Will for you, at which point your decision is already made.

But once again, the ego rises in protest. "Turn over my life *and* my will? You've got to be joking! My will is *mine*!

It belongs to me, no one else. Without it, I'm lost!" But if your will and God's are dissimilar in any way, then you have chosen to separate yourself from God even as you ask Him for help. To turn your will over to God implies nothing more than acknowledging that, as the Course says, "*There is no Will but God's.*"[16] What you regarded as your own private will was just the ego. You cannot treasure it and still hope to find sanity. Your individual will is that unreliable guide through the mountains. Follow it and you are truly lost. Realign your will with Holy Spirit's and you will safely pass by any obstacle.

*   *   *

Seen with the eyes of ego, A.A.'s first three steps appear to be asking a great sacrifice—to give up what's most precious to us: alcohol for the alcoholic, or, for the Course student, the far greater sacrifice of the entire world along with the very notion of who you are. And indeed, that is exactly what is asked! But the sacrifice of illusions is no sacrifice. Nothing is being lost or taken away except dreams. We are awakening to sanity. And to surrender the "will" of the ego, which has no real power, to the Will of God and Holy Spirit, which brings us eternal peace and joy, is hardly a loss. We give up nothing but our chains. We are not asked to surrender our freedom; we are asked to surrender *to* freedom. We clear the dross from our minds in order to make them a clean, open space—an altar upon which we can receive Spirit and its miracles.

The Genesis of Miracles

On its very first page, *A Course in Miracles* states, "*Miracles are natural. When they do not occur something has gone wrong.*"[17] Now we understand, the thing that's "gone wrong"—the obstacle that blocks miracles—is our insanity, that is, our continuing identification with the ego as self. The very fact that miracles are so rare (why else would we call them miracles?) merely testifies to the ego's dominance.

The ego interprets miracles in accordance with its thought system. If one occurs, something special must have taken place to cause it. You uttered the right prayer, worshipped at the right shrine, bowed to the right spiritual leader, called upon the proper angels, and so on. Or you are special, different from other people, handpicked by God. But if miracles are natural, then such explanations are neither necessary nor correct. You are not special. Miracles are available to everyone. And you don't have to do anything to manifest them. They're about undoing, not doing; release instead of action. Your task is simply to get out of the way.

From a Course perspective. then, miracles are not "miraculous," not in the usual sense. They are less a divine intervention than a realignment brought about by the recognition that your will and the Holy Spirit's are not and never were in conflict. Miracles transcend the ego's cause-and-effect paradigm. They offer living proof that it is wrong. When we remove "*the blocks to the awareness of love's presence,*"[18] Ever-Mind comes pouring through, bringing with it miracles.

*   *   *

Imagine a beautiful, clear mountain stream winding its way over smooth rocks and pebbles, swirling to fill deep forest pools, tumbling in a playful cascade of white water as it flows steadily downhill, as it's done for centuries. Now imagine that a construction company begins excavation to build a lodge alongside the stream. A mining company starts digging nearby for gold. A timber outfit clear-cuts the surrounding forest. Trash and debris, sludge and saw-dust are dumped in the water, choking off its flow. Water still manages to seep through in places, but so slowly that it's hardly noticeable. The stream no longer bears any re-semblance to its original nature.

To revive the stream and restore it to its former self, the obstacles to the flow of water must be removed. Debris must be cleaned out, fallen tree trunks lifted, plastic food wrappers dredged out, by hand if necessary. In some places the blockage may be so extreme that only a bulldozer can plow through and clear a new channel.

At first, this is arduous, time-consuming work. There's so much to undo. It's overwhelming. Progress appears halt-ing. But as the water finds its path downhill and begins to flow again, it naturally assists in its own restoration. The brisker the current, the better able it is to carry off waste. Once it's flowing freely again, the stream becomes self-sustaining. It cannot be obstructed except through pur-poseful effort.

The beautiful stream represents the flow of miracles from the Holy Spirit to you. The debris that clutters and blocks its flow are the thoughts of Never-Mind: its fear-driven preoccupations and plans. To the extent that you believe you know better than God—that your judgment trumps the Holy Spirit's—you clog the stream and impede its flow, until finally it stops altogether. At that point, you experience no miracles. They are still there, like the water, but dammed up, unable to penetrate the dense sludge of your ego thoughts. As a result, you become convinced that there is no such thing as a miracle. It does not exist and therefore can't help you. You're alone in life, as you've always been. Only by your own careful planning (and a dash of luck) do you have any shot at happiness.

Of course, you have no chance of cleaning up that stream by yourself, any more than a solitary alter in DID can bring about integration. It was, after all, your own mind that fouled the water and blocked its flow in the first place. How can that same mind, entangled in separation and conflict, ever hope to reverse the damage wrought by its very nature?

It's a bit like trying to sweep dirt out your house using a mud-caked broom. You need a new, clean broom—only you have no idea what that looks like. Do they even exist? You've used a muddy broom all your life, handed down by your parents, and their parents before them. Muddy brooms are what you've got, so you deal with the situation as best you can by sweeping one pile of dirt out of the way, not realizing that in the process you leave another behind. Such is the life of Never-Mind: the ego's Sisyphean game of whack-a-mole.

You need professional cleaners whose job it is to locate the piles of dirt wherever they may be hiding, point them out to you, and then, with your consent, clean them up. These professionals arrive with their own set of sparkling clean brooms, mops, cleansers, rags, and—miracle of miracles—a vacuum cleaner! Invite the Holy Spirit's cleaning service into your house, and He will illuminate for you the layers of dirt and grime created by your thoughts, but overlooked by you, because you considered them normal. And then, with your approval, He will clean them up for you. Dirt vanishes, leaving no trace that it ever was. Everything sparkles. And that is a miracle.

A Better Way

A Course in Miracles came into the world in direct response to a call for help from a man named Bill Thetford, an associate professor of medical psychology at the Columbia College of Physicians and Surgeons in New York. Bill and his close associate, Helen Schucman, fought constantly over just about everything. The intensely competitive academic environment in which they worked only heightened their conflict. One day, for no apparent reason, Bill decided he'd had enough. He declared to Helen that "there must be another way" to relate to each other and their work, and that he was determined to find it. Much to his surprise, and her own, Helen replied, "I will help you." Three months later, in October 1965, as if in answer to Bill's plea, Helen heard an inner Voice that dictated the words: "This is a course in miracles. Please take notes." The scribing of the Course had begun.

Bill had looked at his life and recognized that he and Helen were trapped in a pattern of emotional dysfunction that was neither healthy nor necessary, and that it needed to stop. In Twelve-Step parlance, Bill had hit bottom. He made a commitment to find another, better way to conduct his relationships, and his decision touched his colleague as well. Together they embarked on the journey that was to become *A Course in Miracles*. Unwittingly at first, they had invited the Holy Spirit into their lives to clean house, so to speak. We could also say that two alter personalities going by the names Helen and Bill decided to share a common purpose and walk together down the road to integration.

When Bill made his appeal, he had no idea how his life would change—that he would soon take early retirement and move to California, adopting a whole new lifestyle and a new group of friends in the process of quietly becoming the Course's first teacher. When we invite the Holy Spirit into our lives, we do indeed relinquish control as we knew it. We are led to people and situations that we never could have imagined. And that turns out to be a good thing, because had we known what lay ahead, we would have run from it in fear. But the Course is very clear: the Holy Spirit will never lead us into anything that would cause fear. That would be counterproductive to His mission. In fact, it would be impossible. Love cannot give rise to fear. The two are antithetical. Fear is a response to the separation. It can only exist if we identify with Never-Mind as a separate self. It has no place within the oneness of Ever-Mind.

Fear is a stranger to the ways of love. Identify with fear, and you will be a stranger to yourself. . . . There is no home [that] can shelter fear and love. They cannot coexist. If you are real, then fear must be illusion. And if fear is real, then you do not exist at all.[19]

*   *   *

As we saw in the very first chapter, our false construct of self maintains fear and prevents us from finding happiness. We cannot free ourselves from our emotional blocks because they are too rooted in our notion of self. When we accept that "there must be a better way" and *"step back and let Him lead the way,"*[20] then we are helped along the road to our true Self, the Ever-Mind, through miracles.

Novelist Thomas Pynchon wrote that a miracle is "another world's intrusion into this one."[21] That "other world" operates under a different set of laws, which do not fit with those we know; therefore it will appear miraculous to us. The overlap of that world with ours results in miracles, which by their very presence prove that there must be something more, something beyond the world of the senses. Miracles undermine the absolute faith we placed in the laws of Never-Mind.

Unless we are prepared, however—unless we have intentionally invited this world and its new laws into our world, as Bill and Helen did—then it will indeed feel like an intrusion. It will unbalance us and scare us. This is the risk posed by psychedelic drugs and premature spiritual awakenings. They can overwhelm the mind and produce fear. As a result, the insights they offer remain unheeded. Instead of opening us to love, the fearful experience drives us back into the arms of the ego in hopes of restoring sanity and order. But the ego is incapable of this. It is the poster child for insanity and disorder. Only the Holy Spirit can restore true order.

> *It will seem difficult for you to learn that you have no basis at all for ordering your thoughts. This lesson the Holy Spirit teaches by giving you the shining example of miracles to show you that your way of ordering is wrong, but that a better way is offered you.*[22]

Miracles are that "better way" that Bill Thetford was determined to find. And through *A Course in Miracles*, anyone can learn how to bring them about.

*   *   *

In the summer of 2016, I retired from the practice of psychiatry in order to take on a leadership role with the Foundation for Inner Peace, the original publisher and translator of *A Course in Miracles*. This necessitated moving from New Jersey, where my family and I had lived for eighteen years, back to California, where the Foundation is based. Although we had anticipated the move a good year in advance, there was an enormous amount of work to be done, including closing my office (and in the process saying goodbye to scores of people I'd worked with in therapy for many years, people I'd come to know well and love), getting our house ready to go on the market, and finding a place to live in California, not to mention my son graduating from high school and applying to college.

We decluttered, giving away clothing, furniture, and books by the boxload. We stripped wallpaper, repainted, installed new carpeting, planted flowers and bushes, re-paired those items in need of repair—all at a significant cost in time, money, and energy. We'd met with three different realtors, all of whom gave the same estimate of how much our house would likely sell for. The sluggish condition of the local real-estate market made that signifi-cantly less than we'd planned for, especially since we'd be looking to buy in much pricier Marin County, north of San Francisco. The realtors pointed out that there were a number of houses on the market comparable to ours. The darling home in which we'd invested so much was not the standout we believed it to be; we shouldn't expect a great offer, much less a bidding war. The realtors also suggested rather strongly that we should get our house listed by late March or early April at the latest to take full advantage of the spring market.

Early April came and went, and we were not even close to being ready to list the house. There was just too much to do. Every time our panic level started to rise, we'd remind ourselves that we were doing the best we could. And we im-plicitly trusted that this move was right for us, and there-fore, we had faith that somehow, with the help of Holy Spirit, it would all work out. We weren't exactly counting on miracles, but my decades-long involvement with the Course had shown me firsthand how frequently miracles turned out to be the answer to what looked like an insur-mountable roadblock. (I recount some examples of these in my book *From Plagues to Miracles*.)

We were now in early May. Two more weeks and we'd be flying to San Francisco for ten days with the mission of finding and buying a house. It would sure help if we knew how much we had to spend. Yet we continued to stay calm. This was out of our hands. When I'd lay awake at night churning the "what if" disaster scenarios—what if we got only lowball offers on our house, what if we got no offers, what if we had to put everything in storage and live for a time with our dogs out of a small apartment—I would remind myself to shut up, step back, and turn the whole mess over to the Holy Spirit.

There were bright spots. I had accepted a writing assignment to synopsize the Course for another non-profit, for which they were paying me a very generous sum. There were also glitches, like the discovery—coming on a Friday evening, of course—that our septic tank was close to overflowing because of a failed pump and we'd better stop flushing toilets immediately. The contractors who repaired it two days later overbilled us for their time. And performed the job incorrectly. And so on.

At last the house was ready, or as ready as it would ever be. We were within days of signing a contract with the realtor who seemed the most knowledgeable. My son was out walking when our new neighbors, a couple with young kids (just as we had been when we purchased our house), called him over. "Are your parents thinking of selling their house?" they asked. They had noticed all the contractors—how could they not? He said yes, we were. Some close friends of theirs had been looking to buy in the neighborhood. Would we be open to showing them the house? Um, yes!

They came by that same night. They loved the house and all we'd done with it. The next day they made us a very respectable offer—significantly higher than what the realtors had told us to expect. Plus, we would not have to pay our half of the commission. Just like that, the primary obstacle to moving had cleared. We found a house in Marin that we loved. It was bigger than anticipated, with an unusually large yard for the area. Yes, it was pricier than we'd hoped, but with the extra money from our New Jersey sale, we could just swing it.

I'd like to say the move proceeded smoothly from there on, but it did not. It was harrowing. Yet each time an obstacle arose—and there were many, one in particular with the potential to sink our deal—we would step back and turn it over. And each time, a solution presented itself. Sometimes they were comical, like the time I misread a text from a friend in Marin as coming from our mortgage broker and concluded that our mortgage application was about to go belly-up. Other times, the solution arrived in a flurry of activity at the last possible moment, as in our dealings with the New Jersey Department of Environmental Protection over the removal of an in-ground oil tank. But writing now from Marin on a gorgeous California afternoon, with a garage still laden with boxes and furniture, I can say that all turned out well.

There is a back story to all this. In 1991, my ex-wife and I sold our house outside Philadelphia to move to the Bay Area. The house had sat vacant on the market for six months with our anxiety escalating by the day, at which point we consulted a feng shui master. He gave us a series of rituals to perform. Within five days we had a solid buyer who for some reason was willing to overlook the house's obvious issues. It was all rather remarkable, magical even. But it felt like a spiritual bailout—one for which I was grateful, to be sure, but in which I was not the active agent. Nor was it rooted in the teachings of the Course. Therefore, despite the obvious temptation, I felt strongly guided not to use any similar feng shui "magic" with this house sale.

The point I hope to make here above all others is that my wife and I did not sit down and consciously request a miracle. We never decided up front what we thought should take place. We didn't come up with a dollar amount for our sale or a picture of what our new house in California should look like and then visualize it, pray for it, or employ rituals to bring it about. We simply turned each obstacle over to the Holy Spirit—that Higher Power of A.A.—and trusted, and followed guidance.

As I look back, it does indeed feel miraculous that we were able to accomplish all that was necessary to make the move. In the spring of 2016, I was staring up at a steep mountain range, knowing I had to make the crossing and having no idea how that would happen, or if I'd even make it. The following spring, I look back at those same jagged, snow-capped peaks and find them no less daunting. But I view them now from the other side, knowing that the ascent was rough, but that I did made it across, although I'm still not sure how it all transpired—almost as if I'd been gently lifted up and carried over. And perhaps I was.

I suspect it's a bit like a woman about to give birth. Before labor starts, she has no idea what's involved. Despite all her reading and childbirth classes, despite the stories from other women, there's really no way she can know what she's about to go through. Then the contractions begin, and they're so painful, she's not sure she's going to make it. As they intensify and grow more frequent, she is certain she won't survive. There's no way forward, but no turning back either. The pain builds to a crescendo, she pushes and pushes, exhausted, with seemingly no end in sight, and then, miracle of miracles, the pain is gone and . . . she has a new baby. She had no choice but to trust the process and allow it to unfold.

Similarly, we have to get out of Holy Spirit's way and trust, even if our egos fearfully protest that we're headed down the wrong path. Only by letting go of our own plans and aligning with Ever-Mind and Holy Spirit will we receive the help we truly need.

> *Once you accept [God's] plan as the one function you would fulfill, there will be nothing else the Holy Spirit will not arrange for you without your effort. He will go before you making straight your path and leaving in your way no stones to trip on, and no obstacles to bar your way. Nothing you need will be denied you. Not one seeming difficulty but will melt away before you reach it. You need take thought for nothing, careless of everything except the only purpose that you would fulfill. As that was given you, so will its fulfillment be.[23]*

No Order of Difficulty

When we surrender our agenda to the Holy Spirit in recognition of the fact that the Ever-Mind is our true Self, not the ego, we open a path to miracles. But the majority of these miracles will not be show-stoppers. Some people would not even consider them miraculous. They are not special-effects extravaganzas, nor are they meant to make converts of anyone. They are for us alone; only we can deem them miraculous or not.

Miracles remove obstacles in order to expedite learning. They clear the way, whether that requires the parting of the Red Sea or something far more mundane.

*   *   *

I sat on the deck of a large ferryboat headed for a working vacation. The wind whipped across the deck with such force that I snugged my hat down tight over my head in hopes that it wouldn't be blown away over the side rail and down into the ocean below. In a week's time, I was to lead a three-day workshop on *A Course in Miracles* and I still had a lot to do to prepare. But at the moment, it could wait. I'd abandoned cell phone and laptop in the car belowdecks, intent on simply relaxing and enjoying the trip.

I closed my eyes. The sun and wind, the motion of the boat scudding across the mild ocean swells, lulled me into a deeply peaceful state. It wasn't quite a perfect moment, but Ever-Mind hovered close by. That's when an important idea for the workshop unexpectedly popped into my head. I opened my eyes and grabbed my pen to write it down—but I had no paper. I looked around for a stray magazine or newspaper, hoping someone had left one in my vicinity. Nothing. No paper anywhere. I'd just have to try to remember it. With a smile, I accepted the situation—but paper sure would've been nice. So I closed my eyes for a moment and asked for help.

The wind gusted. From out of nowhere, a tiny scrap of paper danced across the deck and lodged itself right under the sole of my shoe. I snagged it. It was a ticket stub for the ferry. There was just enough blank space on one side for me to jot down my idea and pocket it. And then say, "Thank you."

I have no doubt that in that moment I received a miracle. It was not a big deal. Life and death did not hang in the balance. But perhaps that's the point, and this miracle becomes all the more powerful a demonstration as a result. I had encountered an obstacle: lack of paper to write down an important idea that would benefit my workshop attendees. I needed help and silently asked for it. The obstacle was removed.

* * *

The first of the Course's fifty Principles of Miracles, found at the very beginning of the Text, states:

> *There is no order of difficulty in miracles. One is not "harder" or "bigger" than another. They are all the same. All expressions of love are maximal.*[24]

As these are the opening lines of the Course, if we want to understand miracles, it will be worth our while to examine them in some depth.

First, what exactly is meant by "order of difficulty"? Difficulty is a relative concept belonging to the world of perception. To determine that one thing is harder than another requires making a judgment, and judgment is an ego function. It has no relation to the Ever-Mind. What could be difficult or easy, bigger or smaller, more or less, when all is one forever?

If miracles come from Holy Spirit, not the ego, then miracles cannot obey the ego's laws. Ever. In any way. It's just not possible for one to be bigger or harder than another. Nor can they be compared side by side as we might do with two paintings or two glasses of wine from different vintages to determine which we like better. Miracles are not about scale or quantity. No preference is involved. They are our passage through the mountains, whether that turns out to be an easy summer's day jaunt or a grueling Himalayan ascent.

Miracles are not in competition, and the number of them that you can do is limitless. They can be simultaneous and legion. This is not difficult to understand, once you conceive of them as possible at all. What is more difficult to grasp is the lack of order of difficulty that stamps the miracle as something that must come from elsewhere, not from here. From the world's viewpoint, this is impossible.[25]

Miracles arise as a uniform response to a very specific set of circumstances. The specificity comes from us; the uniformity, from the Holy Spirit. We see our lives bedeviled by a host of troubles, all of them different. He sees only one: the belief that our minds are in any way separate from God. When we are willing to give our seemingly different troubles to the Holy Spirit to solve, we return them to Truth. The Holy Spirit lends us His interpretation of the problem and thereby places it under God's laws instead of the ego's.

This has two results. First, it shows us that our myriad problems can be reduced down to one. And second, it resolves those problems by recognizing that they were never real in the first place. But this occurs only if we allow the "intrusion of another world"—that of Holy Spirit and Ever-Mind—into our perception.

Because the Holy Spirit does not recognize our problems as real, He does not try to solve them at the level where they seem to exist. He sees one problem—the delusional, separated self of Never-Mind—and He sets about correcting it. One problem requires one solution. Therefore, although miracles manifest themselves to us in countless forms tailored to innumerable different circumstances, they are really all the same miracle.

> *The miracle offers exactly the same response to every call for help. It does not judge the call. It merely recognizes what it is, and answers accordingly.*[26]

> *There is one miracle, as there is one reality. And every miracle you do contains them all, as every aspect of reality you see blends quietly into the one reality of God.*[27]

Miracles are holographic. Each one contains all others, because in truth they are one and the same, as all things in God's reality must be. Light may stream through many different windows of varying shapes and sizes, but it is all the same light; whichever window it happens to come through, it banishes darkness with equal efficacy. Each miracle that comes to us unmasks another window onto eternity and helps dispel the ego's shadowy gloom. Each casts that much more light upon our true nature until, finally, we can see it clearly and embrace it. That is the miracle's ultimate purpose—to restore us to our right mind, to Ever-Mind, to God.

Miracle Principle 1 states that miracles are *"all the same,"* but it does not stop there. In the next line, it explains why this is so—why it must be so. Miracles, coming as they do from God (through His Agent, the Holy Spirit), are expressions of love, and *"all expressions of love are maximal."*[28] What does this mean?

As we saw in chapter 2, in the ego's world, everything is fragmented. Love is not a constant and it is hardly a given. We don't love universally. We fall in love, love our children (hopefully), our parents (perhaps). We can also love a concept, like country or religion. But none of these forms of love is constant. Love blossoms only under certain special circumstances. Its scope is limited, rarely moving beyond two people and their families. It lasts for a while, then falters. People disappoint us. Parents fall from their godlike pedestals, while children fail our expectations. As a result, according to the Course, we do not know the meaning of real love—not as God loves. To repeat a quote from the previous chapter:

> As [love] is one itself, it looks on all as one. Its meaning lies
> in oneness. And it must elude the mind that thinks of it as

*partial or in part. There is no love but God's, and all of love
is His.*[29]

Love is not partial. It cannot be divided, diluted, unequally
distributed, or destroyed. It makes no comparisons. The
statement from the first miracle principle that "*all expressions of love are maximal*" reaffirms the all-or-nothing nature of love and its reality. Either we love "maximally," as
God does—in which case that love fills all the space there
is—or we do not love at all. OS1 is the system software
of love. In the presence of genuine love, what the Greeks
called *agape*, OS2 crashes. It can't run love.

Because this world is illusion, and because only love is
real, when love—real love, God's love—enters this world,
it changes it. It shifts perception in the direction of oneness, and that is the miracle. Love doesn't need to distinguish among different forms of suffering to heal them all.
Like water, it takes the shape of whatever vessel it's poured
into and fills it completely so we may drink.

Here is one of the best descriptions from the Course of
how love impacts the ego's world of form. Although miracles are not specifically mentioned, it is clear that this is the
mechanism by which they operate.

*[Your Creator's] Voice is calling from the known to the un-
knowing. He would comfort you, although He knows no
sorrow. He would make a restitution, though He is complete; a gift to you, although He knows that you have everything already. He has Thoughts which answer every need
[you] perceive, although He sees them not. For Love must*

give, and what is given in His Name takes on the form most useful in a world of form.[30]

God's Thoughts (which arise from Love and are themselves Love) get refracted into the world of form through the medium of the Holy Spirit. Here they take shape and manifest as miracles. Like purest white light passing through a prism, God's Love beams into the world to become the entire spectrum of potential miracles. They take on different forms, different colors, but all originate from the same Source and in their essence remain unchanged. Light is light. Love is love.

The Ego Strikes Back

Unfortunately, when miracles come our way, the ego also gets busy. It tries to minimize the miracle's impact and divert us from what it would teach us. The ego has several methods for achieving this. It will attempt to explain miracles away as mere chance or good luck. For instance, it would claim that my wife and I simply got lucky when that couple appeared to buy our home. If luck doesn't do the trick, the ego will try to minimize the miracle by explaining it away in terms of its cause-and-effect paradigm. In *From Plagues to Miracles*, I described many miracles and the ego's attempts to undercut them with rationalization, including one particularly powerful experience recounted by Course scribe Helen Schucman in her autobiography.[31]

Helen was visiting the healing shrine of Lourdes with her parents and was very taken by the piles of discarded crutches and proofs of miraculous healings. Inspired by what she'd seen, she prayed to God one night for a miracle. She decided that she would close her eyes, say three Hail Marys, and when she reopened her eyes, she would look for a meteor streaking across the sky. That would be her sign that God had heard her and responded with a miracle. When she opened her eyes, however, Helen witnessed not just one meager meteor, but an entire sky crisscrossed with shooting stars. She was awestruck and ever so grateful to have her proof that God existed and had heard her prayers.

The next day, however, Helen recalled that her tour guide had mentioned the possibility of meteor showers at that time of year. Immediately she discounted what she'd seen. It wasn't a miracle from God after all; it was merely a seasonal meteor shower. She had manipulated it into a faux miracle by choosing as her proof an event that she had already known might occur. Instead of supporting her faith, the experience undermined it. This is the ego at work.

However, the mere fact that a miracle can be explained as a result of natural causes does not detract from its miraculous nature. Miracles are about timing and intention. They respond to a need and arrive at the perfect time to address that need—usually when we reach the point of surrender and ask for help (even if that asking is unconscious). Helen's meteor shower appeared at precisely the instant she closed her eyes and asked—not five minutes earlier or later, when it wouldn't have mattered. We are the only ones who can know the challenges we face; therefore we are the only ones who can say whether or not an event was miraculous, no matter how it might look to the outside world.

There is yet another way the ego can react to a miracle. It is very much the opposite of rationalization, and it is even more destructive. Instead of dismissing the miracle, the ego grabs hold and runs with it. It takes credit for the miracle and uses it to enhance its status relative to other people. The miracle becomes a sign of specialness, whether our own, our football team's, or our religion's.

Of course, this sense of specialness contributes to division and conflict when other groups are deemed as less special and unworthy of miracles. In our DID model, if one alter personality were to proclaim that the therapist loved her best and put forward as proof some loving action by the therapist, the other alters would not take it well. Some would attack or shun her. Others might slink away convinced of their own inferiority. And still others would blame the therapist, rightly or not, for playing favorites. In their anger and spite, they might very well try to sabotage the treatment.

A Course in Miracles cautions that "*the use of miracles as spectacles to induce belief is a misunderstanding of their purpose.*"[32] Miracles are not to be put on display. They are not exhibits in a charismatic tent revival show. Their purpose is not to impress or make converts of unbelievers. They are demonstrations of God's Love for us in whatever form we need most at a given time. And if we choose to share them, as I do here, it should only be to emphasize that we are all equally deserving of them in the eyes of God and the Holy Spirit.

Ordinary Miracles

Miracles are perfectly ordinary in the sense that they are natural and not special. They represent the default response of the Holy Spirit's OS1 to any problem we happen to perceive while running the ego's OS2.

> *You have no problems that [the Holy Spirit] cannot solve by offering you a miracle. Miracles are for you.*[33]

But although they are ordinary, we must never take miracles for granted. And once we have received miracles, the only appropriate response is gratitude.

To say that miracles are ordinary may seem like a contradiction in terms. Aren't miracles by definition extraordinary? To the ego, yes. To Ever-Mind and the Holy Spirit, absolutely not. Their ordinariness is an inextricable aspect of their nature: that they are basically all one and the same; that when it comes to miracles, there is "no order of difficulty."

But as we know, the ego thrives on differences. It revels in comparisons. It can't help itself. Remember, contrast is the very basis of perception. Without it, there is no world to see, hear, or touch. Left to its own devices, then, the ego will compare and, if possible, rank just about everything: the top ten restaurants, doctors, athletes, cities, vacation spots, and so on. The ego judges miracles by how impossible or spectacular they seem to be. This undermines their value as learning devices. If we predetermine that only "big" miracles are worthy of the designation, then the ego will have succeeded at its task. It will have brought "order of difficulty" back into the concept of miracles.

The fact is, we rarely need what the ego would consider a real miracle. How often do life and death truly hang in the balance? How many Red Seas will need to part for us in the course of one lifetime? Miracles aren't just for special occasions. They're everyday. And when we recognize this and practice them daily, then when the big challenges blow into our lives, well, it's just another opportunity for ordinary miracles.

In the biblical books of Exodus and Numbers, the Hebrew people escape from bondage in Egypt only to wander the desolate wilderness for forty years. Nothing grows there; they are sustained only by manna, a mysterious substance that appears with the sunrise to cover the ground, much like morning dew. Manna is edible for a single day only. Try to save or accumulate it, and it rots. One way of understanding this is that manna addresses whatever need, whatever hunger, we happen to have within the confines of a given day.

In *From Plagues to Miracles*, I interpret manna as the generic symbol of miracles, that is, the ordinary, day-to-day miracles that show up in our lives to see us through our own experience of the wilderness. They may not be Hollywood-style extravaganzas like crossing the Red Sea, but then they don't need to be. Like manna, miracles sustain us. Without them, we do not survive.

Buddhist monks go door-to-door every morning asking for food. They are not allowed to accept more than they can consume in the course of one day. Recovering alcoholics are cautioned to engage sobriety one day at a time. Stay sober for the span of a single day—that's all that's asked. Make this your commitment every morning, and you will be sober for a lifetime.

The ego prefers to peer far into the future. It seeks out the dangers that lie in wait for us and hopes to prepare for them through prudent planning. That's not how miracles work. They can meet us only in the present tense, only now, because that's where we encounter Ever-Mind. *Now* is all there is. It's where we live, even if we forget or pretend not to know it.

The irony is, if we turn our will and our lives over to God, Holy Spirit, Higher Power—if, as we roll out of bed each morning, we establish that as our only goal for the coming day—then all else falls into place and we are guaranteed miracles. The Course says we are *"entitled to miracles"*[34] because of what we are—Christ, God's Son— but we cannot demand or petition for them because to do so instantly reinstates the ego. Nor can we decide which miracle is right for us. What our egos tell us we need and what we really need are opposite in every way. This is why it's so essential to recognize our limits and get out of the way. We get to decide yes or no, OS1 or OS2; the rest is up to the Holy Spirit. *"The power of decision is your one remaining freedom as a prisoner of this world."*[35] If you waste this power by trying to decide which card to pick from the ego's three-card monte scam, you lose the miracle. If you make the one choice that matters, then miracles are yours.

Miracles—Markers of Progress

The ego has us so turned around, so befuddled, that we cannot accurately gauge our progress, or even the direction in which we're headed. This confusion is far worse than any of us realize. We lack the wisdom to know whether we are learning and advancing or falling farther behind.

> *You cannot distinguish between advance and retreat. Some of your greatest advances you have judged as failures, and some of your deepest retreats you have evaluated as success.*[36]

When miracles appear in our lives, they confirm that we're on the right path. They blaze the trail that leads back to God and wholeness, appearing at intervals to let us know we have not strayed, but remain on track.

*   *   *

I once had the opportunity to play amateur copilot to an experienced pilot. We were flying at night to the island of Nantucket in a small, twin-engine prop plane. As we neared our destination, the plane entered a dense fog bank. Our range of vision from the cockpit was choked down almost to nothing. In order to land safely, we had to be able to see the runway lights. We circled and circled, straining our eyes for a glimpse of them. For the slimmest fraction of a second, the fog thinned and I spied twin lines of flashing lights arrowing out below us. And then they were gone. The fog had closed back in. I told the pilot and he began his descent. But I didn't fully trust what I'd seen.

Might I have imagined it? Or mistaken the flashing lights of the plane itself reflecting off the fog for runway lights? I voiced my concern, but the pilot shrugged them off. He trusted my vision. The plane dropped steadily through the fog. I tensed, anticipating our collision with the ground, wondering if I'd stay conscious long enough to even register the crash. All of a sudden, we broke through the fog. The runway lights crystallized into sharp clarity directly below us. The pilot touched down on the runway with barely a jolt while I sighed with relief.

Miracles are like that first, fleeting glimmer of runway lights breaking through the fog. When one flashes into your life, you may at first doubt its reality. You may strain in vain to pierce the fog for a repeat glimpse of yet another miracle. But with experience comes trust in your vision. And when miracles do appear, standing out from your everyday experience as brightly and cleanly as those flashing runway lights amidst the foggy darkness, you know you're safe. You know you're almost home.

All for One, One for All

Let's return for a moment to DID as a model of our predicament. We have dissociated from the one Mind of God by fragmenting into billions of seemingly different and separate individual selves: the alter personalities, so to speak, of Ever-Mind. Each human being is an alter; each is in dire need of treatment, whether they know it or not. We all face the daunting task of navigating passage across the mountains. We all play pickup sticks with a gun pressed to the temple, where the outcome of any wrong move can instantly prove fatal. Or so we've been taught to believe.

But we have help. In the Holy Spirit, we have a trustworthy Guide through the mountains and the perfect DID Therapist—perfect because He comes from oneness, yet can perceive duality and division, and serves as a bridge between the two. He reinterprets our fragmented lives in a way that joins us and leads back to oneness. And one of the key tools in his therapeutic toolbox is the miracle.

As Therapist, the Holy Spirit works with each one of us individually, as if we were in fact separate and alone. He brings us miracles (when we let Him) to remove obstacles that stand in the way of oneness. With time, we come to accept His vision of what we are in place of our own, and to embrace His purpose as ours. As a result, we learn that we are not the self we believed ourselves to be, but part of something much greater. And we learn to recognize that same greater Self in everyone. Now our neighbor has indeed become our Self.

> *Those who accept the Holy Spirit's purpose as their own share also His vision. And what enables Him to see His purpose shine forth from every altar now is yours as well as His. He sees no strangers, only dearly loved and loving friends.*[37]

We saw in chapter 4 that no purpose could truly bind the members of a group together unless it was solidly based in truth. The Holy Spirit gives us such a purpose. We become His ambassadors, His extensions (or auxiliary therapists, if you like) when we join with Him in his mission of healing.

At the same time that He works with each of us, the Holy Spirit works with every other alter personality on the planet in exactly the same manner, to the extent that they'll allow it. As we have seen, some alters are more recalcitrant than others. Some gratefully embrace treatment; others resist, sabotage, or try to hide. But no matter their state of readiness, the Holy Spirit views them all as His patients, or more accurately, as aspects of his one and only patient. Because He sees only the oneness within each of us, when He bestows miracles, they may appear to be for us alone. But in reality, they are for everyone. He always serves the collective Self to which we all belong. In this sense, every miracle is an echo of oneness and a movement towards union.

Like an array of tuning forks, when one of us begins to hum with miracles, it is more likely that others around us will pick up the vibration and do the same. As *A Course in Miracles* points out, if someone you know experiences a miracle or has a prayer answered, are you more or less likely to believe that the same could happen to you? Do you think, "Darn, that miracle should have been mine. Now I'll never get to have one"? Or do you think, "Well, if it could happen to them, why not me too?"

If the goal of treatment is integration—unity—then anything that reduces the fear of union in one person will reduce it to some extent in all; any miracle that removes an obstacle in one life makes it more likely that another will allow the same intervention to occur. Resolve the separation at the micro level in your own life and you cannot help but mend the separation at the macro level for the entire collective of humankind. The benefit to one must accrue to all, because in truth they are the same.

One brother is all brothers. Every mind contains all minds, for every mind is one. Such is the truth.[38]

The Games Egos Play

Game theory distinguishes between two fundamentally different types of games: zero-sum and non-zero-sum. In a zero-sum game, the final sum of all moves must add up to zero. What does this mean? There are finite resources (Monopoly properties, poker chips, etc.) and thus, when one player gains, another must lose. I can win only at your expense. By contrast, in a non-zero-sum game, everyone is capable of winning (or losing) together. As a result, zero-sum games are competitive, while non-zero-sum games are collaborative.

It's telling that most board and card games are zero-sum. The ego wants to win, to come out on top, even if that risks the possibility of losing or of making others unhappy. The ego's entire world is one giant zero-sum game. It is populated by individuals, each with her own body and his own separate interests that inevitably clash and come into conflict. What I possess, you lack; what you take for yourself, I must do without. Even if I freely give you something of value, then I no longer have it. This gives rise to the whole notion of sacrifice and the guilt inherent in it, which will be a subject of later books in this series.

Of course, there is a bitter irony underlying the ego's devotion to zero-sum winning. The ego cannot change God's reality, and the nature of that reality is non-zero-sum. Therefore the end result of the ego's striving is not individual triumph but collective loss. Nobody wins! No one gets everything he wanted. No one finds lasting peace or happiness. No one lives forever. At the conclusion of the ego's game, everyone dies. The only winner is death.

By contrast, the Holy Spirit's plan for Atonement (also known as salvation) is clearly and openly non-zero-sum. We're all in it together. Sooner or later, we all wake up from our collective dream. The oneness we regain is eternal. We all win.

> *Salvation can be thought of as a game that happy children play. It was designed by One Who loves His children, and Who would replace their fearful toys with joyous games, which teach them that the game of fear is gone. His game instructs in happiness because there is no loser. Everyone who plays must win, and in his winning is the gain to everyone ensured.*[39]

Whatever serves to bring us closer, whatever rekindles the memory of Ever-Mind, whatever mends the divisions that appear to separate us, will benefit us all. Under the Holy Spirit's therapeutic care, the healing of the individual alter personalities becomes the healing of the whole. We gain both individually and collectively. This broadens the scope of miracles and extends their impact well beyond the boundaries of the personal self. One person's miracle is everyone's gain.

A miracle . . . may touch many people you have not even met, and produce undreamed of changes in situations of which you are not even aware.[40]

You need not realize that healing comes to many brothers far across the world, as well as to the ones you see nearby, as you send out these thoughts to bless the world. But you will sense your own release, although you may not fully understand as yet that you could never be released alone.[41]

Again we see how little we know, and how important it is to the Holy Spirit's treatment plan that we understand and accept our limits. We are each a small, but essential, piece of the collective Self. The Holy Spirit is working to heal that Self in all its parts and aspects, all its forms and manifestations. He will take any opening we give Him and use it to bring darkness into the light, division into unity.

Our task is not to leap into action on His behalf. He doesn't need us for that; He's fully capable. He asks only that we let Him into our lives so that He can do His job. The Course tells us that our own self-initiated attempts to improve the world are misguided. However well-intended, they are guaranteed to backfire, because they target the wrong thing. They address the effect and not its cause. They try to change illusions without changing the mind that spins the illusions.

Therefore, seek not to change the world, but choose to change your mind about the world. Perception is a result and not a cause. And that is why order of difficulty in miracles is meaningless.[42]

The world is an effect, a consequence of running the Never-Mind's OS2. You cannot change the effect without addressing its source, which is our collective case of DID: the separation from God. And that's the Holy Spirit's job because He sees the big picture and you don't. You can't.

Instead of trying to change the world, the Course instructs us that our only job—the only thing we need to focus on—is to manage our own chaotic minds and bring them to the Holy Spirit for healing.

The sole responsibility of the miracle worker is to accept the Atonement for himself.[43]

Change your mind, accept the Holy Spirit's master plan for the healing of all the separated ones, follow His guidance, and you have done your part. You have changed the world in the only way possible. It is not your job to understand how this will occur, much less to evaluate its progress or effectiveness. That's well above your pay grade, or mine. It is enough to know that you have played your part, and in so doing, you have made it possible for others to play theirs and join you in the shared goal of reuniting the separated Children of God.

Everyone in the world must play his part in its redemption, in order to recognize that the world has been redeemed.[44]

According to the Course, this is the way the world ends: not with a bang, nor with a whimper, but in light, love and laughter, as time and space give way to an endless, shared perfect moment. That's what awaits us when we shed Never-Mind for Ever-Mind and reawaken to our true Self in God.

Author's Note

This book is the first in a series of five books devoted to bringing the principles of *A Course in Miracles* to the general reader. Books 2 and 3 will look more deeply into the Course's teachings on forgiveness, specialness, relationships, guilt, attack, defenses, sacrifice, love, the body, sickness and healing, death, vision, giving and receiving, and the holy instant. Book 4 will use a Q&A format to discuss common misunderstandings about the Course and controversial topics like the role of sex and money in the life of the Course student. Book 5 will offer something entirely different: a summary of all that came before, and yet also a completely new approach to the Course's central teaching that *nothing real can be threatened. Nothing unreal exists. Herein lies the peace of God.*

If you would like to learn more about *A Course in Miracles (ACIM)*, please visit the website of the Foundation for Inner Peace, publisher of the Course and its translations, at www.acim.org. There you can also find information about the Course's history and answers to many questions you might have. Should you decide to purchase the Course, you will discover that there are several different editions available. I strongly recommend the Combined Edition with the blue cover published by our Foundation. This is the most popular. It is also the edition used and approved by ACIM's two scribes, Helen Schucman and Bill Thetford. The others, including the so-called "original" ACIM and the annotated edition, are based on earlier rough drafts which some students prefer, but which can be confusing for newer students.

Acknowledgments

I would like to thank and acknowledge Dan Strutzel for approaching me with this writing assignment from Spirit and everyone at G&D Media for helping to bring it to fruition. I am also grateful to my editor, Richard Smoley, whom I have admired since his *Gnosis* magazine days. It's an honor and a pleasure to have you on my team. And finally, my gratitude to all of those with whom I've sat in Miracles groups over the decades, sharing, listening, learning, and teaching together. You have no idea how much you've contributed to this book series and how you've helped me to step into my present role in the *Course in Miracles* community. I am honored to count you among my mighty companions.

Endnotes

The references to quotes from *A Course in Miracles* follow the annotation system developed by the Foundation for A Course in Miracles (FACIM) and widely used throughout the Course community. In deference to readers who may have no experience with the Course, however, I have chosen to spell out the names Text, Workbook, Manual for Teachers, Clarification of Terms, and Song of Prayer in their entirety instead of abbreviating them. I have also indicated Workbook Lessons rather than citing them only by their number as FACIM does. Finally, I have used commas for all volumes for the sake of uniformity rather than dashes before chapter numbers in the Text.

So, for example:
Note 2: Text, 22.VI.1:8–9 refers to the Text's chapter 22, section VI, paragraph 1, lines 8–9.
Note 31: Workbook, Lesson 132.4:1–2, 5:1–2 refers to Lesson 132, lines 1–2 in both paragraph 4 and paragraph 5.

Note 112: Workbook, part II, 13.2:3–4 refers to paragraph 2, lines 3–4 in section 13 of part II of the Workbook, which falls between Lessons 340 and 341.

Note 34: Manual for Teachers, 10.3:1–4:5 refers to section 10 in the Manual, paragraph 3, line 1 through paragraph 4, line 5 inclusive.

Note 38: Clarification of Terms, 6.4:1–10 refers to section 6 in the Clarification of Terms, paragraph 4, lines 1–10.

Introduction

1   *A Course in Miracles,* 3d ed. (Mill Valley, CA: Foundation for Inner Peace, 2007), Text, Introduction, 2.1–3. In further references *A Course in Miracles* will be abbreviated as ACIM.

Chapter 1

1   ACIM, Text, 22.VI.1:8–9.
2   ACIM, Workbook, Lesson 71.4:3.
3   ACIM, Text, 2.I.3:6.
4   Ibid., 8.III.5:1–2.
5   Ibid., 16.III.4:1.
6   Ibid., 21.I, subhead.
7   ACIM, Workbook, Lesson 139.3:1.
8   Ibid., Lesson 139.1:4–6.
9   William Shakespeare, *Romeo and Juliet*, act 2, scene 2, 43–44.
10 ACIM, Workbook, Lesson 128.3:2–3.

11   ACIM, Text, 31.VII.7:1.

12   ACIM, Clarification of Terms, 2.2:2, 3:1

13   William Shakespeare, *Macbeth*, act 5, scene 5, 24–28.

14   ACIM, Workbook, Lesson 188.1:2–4.

15   Robert Rosenthal, *From Plagues to Miracles: The Transformational Journey of Exodus, from the Slavery of Ego to the Promised Land of Spirit* (Carlsbad, CA: Hay House, 2012), 32–33.

16   ACIM, Workbook, Lesson 49.1:2–2:2.

17   ACIM, Workbook, Lesson 93.5:1–5, 9.

18   ACIM, Text, 5.V.6:6–10.

Chapter 2

1   ACIM, Text, 21.V.1:1–2.

2   Ibid., 21.II.9:5.

3   https://www.youtube.com/watch?v=vJG698U2Mvo, published March 10, 2010, copyright 1999 by Daniel J. Simmons

4   ACIM, Text, 24.VI.9:2.

5   ACIM, Manual for Teachers, 8.1:1–7.

6   ACIM, Workbook, Lesson 7.3:1–7.

7   ACIM, Text, 7.VI.7:7.

8   Ibid., 24.VII.8:8–10.

9   Ibid., 15.V.1:7.

10   ACIM, Workbook, Lesson 132.4:1–2, 5:1–2.

11   ACIM, Text, Introduction, 1:4–5.

12   Ibid., 3.V.7:7–8:4.

13   ACIM, Manual for Teachers, 10.3:1–4:5.

14   Ibid., 4.III.1:2–3.

15   ACIM Text, 29.IX.2:1–5

16 ACIM Workbook, Review V. Intro.4:3 (and others)

17 ACIM, Clarification of Terms, 6.4:1–10.

18 ACIM, Text,14.IV.5:2.

19 ACIM, Manual for Teachers, 10.4:7–5:1.

20 ACIM, Text,16.II.9:1–3.

21 Ibid., 14.III.16:1–2.

22 William Shakespeare, *As You Like It*, act 2, scene 7, 139–142.

23 ACIM, Workbook, Lesson 304.1:3–4.

24 Produced by David Catlin and the Chicago Looking-Glass Alice Theatre Company.

25 ACIM, Workbook, Lesson 56.4:2–6.

26 Ibid., Lessons 7 and 9.

27 Ibid., Lesson 184.1:2–2:2.

Chapter 3

1 Fr. John-Julian, ed., *The Compete Julian of Norwich* (Brewster, MA: Paraclete, 2009), 149.

2 Eugene O'Neill, *Long Day's Journey Into Night* (New Haven, CT: Yale University Press, 1955), 153.

3 ACIM, Workbook, Lesson 164.4:1–2.

4 Ibid., Lesson 44.10:2.

5 Ibid., Lesson 108.2:1–3.

6 ACIM, Text, 13.VI.11:1–8.

7 Ibid., 18.VIII.8:1–3.

8 Anne Taves, *Revelatory Events: Three Case Studies of the Emergence of New Spiritual Paths* (Princeton, NJ: Princeton University Press, 2016), 99.

9 ACIM, Text, 18.VI.11:1–11.

10 ACIM, Text, Introduction, 1:7.

11   ACIM, Workbook, Lesson 158.7:1–5.

12   Ibid., Lesson 29.3:1–5.

13   Ibid., Lesson 30.2:3–5,4:1,5:1–2.

14   ACIM, Text, 18.VI.11:7–9.

Chapter 4

1   ACIM, Text, 4.II.2:1–2.

2   Sebastian Junger, *Tribe: On Homecoming and Belonging* (London: HarperCollins, 2016), 9.

3   Ibid., 9–10.

4   Ibid., 14–15.

5   ACIM, Text, 23.IV.7:4.

6   Ibid., 16.II.4:3.

7   Ibid., 12.IV.1:4. Emphasis in the original.

8   John Milton, *Paradise Lost*, 1.263.

9   ACIM, Text, 14.X.10:7.

10   Ibid., 21.VII.13:1.

11   Ibid., 22.II.3:5–6.

12   Ibid., 29.VII.1:1–2

13   Ibid., 26.VI.1:1–2, 7.

14   ACIM, Workbook, Lesson 318.1:2–3.

15   Ibid., Lesson 100.1:3.

16   ACIM, Text, 13.VII.17:1.

17   *The Song of Prayer*, 1, introduction.1:2–3. (This text can be found in ACIM, 3d ed.)

18   ACIM, Text, 14.V.5:1.

Chapter 5

1   ACIM, Text, 12.VII.8:1.

2   Ibid., 12.II.3:3–5

3   "Mr. Potato Head," Classic Toy Museum website; https://burlingamepezmuseum.com/classictoy/potato.html, accessed Sept. 8, 2017.

4   ACIM, Text, 14.VII.4:3–5.

5   Ibid., 10.II.1:2–6.

6   ACIM, Workbook, Lesson 95.2:2.

7   Ibid., Lesson 136.3:1–2.

8   Ibid., Lesson 100.1:2.

9   ACIM, Text, 22.II.6:6–7.

10   ACIM, Workbook, Lesson 318.1:2–3.

11   ACIM, Text, 25.I.4:3–4.

12   Ibid., 9.IV.1:4–6.

13   ACIM Workbook, Lesson 262.1:1–5, 7–8

14   ACIM Text, 24.VI.7:1.

15   ACIM, Workbook, Lesson 67.

16   Ibid., Lesson 229.

17   Ibid., Lesson 127.3:2–8

18   ACIM, Text, 26.VII.9:1–2.

19   Ibid., 14.X.10:5–6.

20   ACIM, Workbook, Lessons 94, 110, 112, 120, 162, 176.

21   Ibid., Lesson 318.1:5–7.

22   ACIM Text, 28.IV.8:1–3, 9:5–7

23   Ibid., Lesson 243.2:3.

Chapter 6

1   ACIM, Text, 1.I.6:1.

2   ACIM, Workbook, Lesson 96.3:1–5.

3   ACIM, Text, 25.I.5:1–2.

4   ACIM, Workbook, part II, 13.2:3–4.

5   ACIM, Text, 12.VII.3:2–3.

6   ACIM Workbook, Lesson 155.10:4–6.

7   Ibid, Lesson 215.1:2–4

8   Alcoholics Anonymous, *Twelve Steps and Twelve Traditions* (New York: Alcoholics Anonymous, 1952), 21, 25, 34.

9   ACIM, Text, 24.II.14:2.

10 Ibid., 2.III.3:5–6.

11 Ibid., 26.II.1:5–7

12 ACIM, Workbook, Lessons 3, 5, 10, 24, and 25.

13 ACIM, Text, 14.XI.6:7–9.

14 Ibid., 31.V.17:7.

15 ACIM, Workbook, Part II, 4.1:1–3.

16 Ibid., Lesson 74.

17 ACIM, Text,1.I.6:1–2.

18 ACIM, Text, Introduction, 1:7.

19 ACIM, Workbook, Lesson 160.1:1–2; 4:5–8.

20 Ibid., Lesson 155.

21 Thomas Pynchon, *The Crying of Lot 49* (Philadelphia: Bantam, 1966), 88.

22 ACIM, Text, 14.X.6:1–2.

23 Ibid., 20.IV.8:4–9.

24 Ibid., 1.I.1:1–4.

25 Ibid., 14.X.3:1–5.

26 Ibid., 14.X.6:3–5.

27 Ibid., 13.VIII.6:3–4.

28 Ibid., 1.I.1.4.

29 ACIM, Workbook, Lesson 127.3:2–5.

30 Ibid., Lesson 186.13:1–5. Emphasis mine.

31   Robert Skutch, *Journey Without Distance: The Story Behind A Course in Miracles* (Berkeley, CA: Celestial Arts, 1984) 17–19

32   ACIM, Text, 1.I.10.

33   Ibid., 14.XI.9:2–3.

34   ACIM, Workbook, Lesson 77.

35   ACIM, Text, 12.VII.9:1.

36   Ibid., 18.V.1:5–6.

37   Ibid., 20.II.5:3–5.

38   ACIM, Workbook, Lesson 161.4:1–3.

39   ACIM, Workbook, Lesson 153.12:1–4.

40   ACIM, Text,1.I.45:1–2.

41   ACIM, Workbook, Lesson 132.16:1–2.

42   ACIM, Text, 21.Introduction.1:7–9.

43   Ibid., 2.V.5:1.

44   Ibid., 12.VII.2:1.

Printed in the USA
CPSIA information can be obtained
at www.ICGtesting.com
JSHW012020140824
68134JS00033B/2792